C
Pocket Reference

C
Pocket Reference

Peter Prinz and Ulla Kirch-Prinz

Translated by Tony Crawford

O'REILLY®

Beijing · Cambridge · Farnham · Köln · Sebastopol · Taipel · Tokyo

C Pocket Reference
by Peter Prinz and Ulla Kirch-Prinz

Published by O'Reilly Media, Inc., 1005 Gravenstein Highway North,
Sebastopol, CA 95472.

O'Reilly Media, Inc. books may be purchased for educational,
business, or sales promotional use. Online editions are also available
for most titles (*safari.oreilly.com*). For more information, contact our
corporate/institutional sales department: (800) 998-9938 or
corporate@oreilly.com.

Editor:	Jonathan Gennick
Production Editor:	Jane Ellin
Cover Designer:	Pam Spremulli
Interior Designer:	David Futato

Printing History:

November 2002:	First Edition.

ISBN: 978-0-596-00436-1
[TM]

Contents

C Pocket Reference

Introduction

The programming language C was developed in the 1970s by Dennis Ritchie at Bell Labs (Murray Hill, New Jersey) in the process of implementing the Unix operating system on a DEC PDP-11 computer. C has its origins in the typeless programming language BCPL (Basic Combined Programming Language, developed by M. Richards) and in B (developed by K. Thompson). In 1978, Brian Kernighan and Dennis Ritchie produced the first publicly available description of C, now known as the K&R standard.

C is a highly portable language oriented towards the architecture of today's computers. The actual language itself is relatively small and contains few hardware-specific elements. It includes no input/output statements or memory management techniques, for example. Functions to address these tasks are available in the extensive C standard library.

C's design has significant advantages:

- Source code is highly portable
- Machine code is efficient
- C compilers are available for all current systems

The first part of this pocket reference describes the C language, and the second part is devoted to the C standard library. The description of C is based on the ANSI X3.159 standard. This standard corresponds to the international standard ISO/IEC 9899, which was adopted by the International Organization for Standardization in 1990, then amended in 1995 and 1999. The ISO/IEC 9899 standard can be ordered from the ANSI web site; see *http://webstore.ansi.org/*.

The 1995 standard is supported by all common C compilers today. The new extensions defined in the 1999 release (called "ANSI C99" for short) are not yet implemented in many C compilers, and are therefore specially labeled in this book. New types, functions, and macros introduced in ANSI C99 are indicated by an asterisk in parentheses (*).

Font Conventions

The following typographic conventions are used in this book:

Italic
    Used to introduce new terms, and to indicate filenames.

Constant width
    Used for C program code as well as for functions and directives.

Constant width italic
    Indicates replaceable items within code syntax.

Constant width bold
    Used to highlight code passages for special attention.

Fundamentals

A C program consists of individual building blocks called *functions*, which can invoke one another. Each function performs a certain task. Ready-made functions are available in the standard library; other functions are written by the programmer as necessary. A special function name is *main()*: this designates the first function invoked when a program starts. All other functions are subroutines.

C Program Structure

Figure 1 illustrates the structure of a C program. The program shown consists of the functions main() and showPage(), and prints the beginning of a text file to be specified on the command line when the program is started.

```
/* Head.c: This program outputs the beginning of a      *
 * text file to the standard output.                     *  Comments
 * Usage : Head <filename>                               */

#include <stdio.h>                          Preprocessor directives
#define LINES        22

void showPage( FILE * );        // prototype      Function main()

int main( int argc, char **argv )
{
        FILE *fp; int exit_code = 0;
        if ( argc != 2 )
        {
                fprintf( stderr, "Usage: Head <filename>\n" );
                exit_code = 1;
        }
        else if ( ( fp = fopen( argv[1], "r" )) == NULL )
        {
                fprintf( stderr, "Error opening file!\n" );
                exit_code = 2;
        }
        else
        {
                showPage( fp );
                fclose( fp );
        }
        return exit_code;
}

void showPage( FILE *fp )       // Output a screen page    Other functions
{
        int count = 0;
        char line[81];
        while ( count < LINES && fgets( line, 81, fp ) != NULL )
        {
                fputs( line, stdout );
                ++count;
        }
}
```

Figure 1. A C program

The *statements* that make up the functions, together with the necessary declarations and preprocessing directives, form the *source code* of a C program. For small programs, the source code is written in a single *source file*. Larger C programs consist of several source files, which can be edited and compiled separately. Each such source file contains functions that belong to a logical unit, such as functions for output to a terminal, for example. Information that is needed in several source files, such as declarations, is placed in header files. These can then be included in each source file via the #include directive.

Source files have names ending in .c; header files have names ending in .h. A source file together with the header files included in it is called a *translation unit*.

There is no prescribed order in which functions must be defined. The function showPage() in Figure 1 could also be placed before the function main(). A function cannot be defined within another function, however.

The compiler processes each source file in sequence and decomposes its contents into *tokens*, such as function names and operators. Tokens can be separated by one or more whitespace characters, such as space, tab, or newline characters. Thus only the order of tokens in the file matters. The layout of the source code—line breaks and indentation, for example—is unimportant. The *preprocessing directives* are an exception to this rule, however. These directives are commands to be executed by the preprocessor before the actual program is compiled, and each one occupies a line to itself, beginning with a hash mark (#).

Comments are any strings enclosed either between /* and */, or between // and the end of the line. In the preliminary phases of translation, before any object code is generated, each comment is replaced by *one* space. Then the preprocessing directives are executed.

Character Sets

ANSI C defines two character sets. The first is the *source character set*, which is the set of characters that may be used in a source file. The second is the *execution character set*, which consists of all the characters that are interpreted during the execution of the program, such as the characters in a string constant.

Each of these character sets contains a *basic character set*, which includes the following:

- The 52 upper- and lower-case letters of the Latin alphabet:

  ```
  A B C D E F G H I J K L M N O P Q R S T U V W X Y Z
  a b c d e f g h i j k l m n o p q r s t u v w x y z
  ```

- The ten decimal digits (where the value of each character after 0 is one greater than the previous digit):

  ```
  0 1 2 3 4 5 6 7 8 9
  ```

- The following 29 graphic characters:

  ```
  !  "  #  %  &  '  (  )  *  +  ,  -  .  /  :  ;
  <  =  >  ?  [  \  ]  ^  _  {  |  }  ~
  ```

- The five whitespace characters:

      space, horizontal tab, vertical tab, newline, form feed

In addition, the basic execution character set contains the following:

- The null character \0, which terminates a character string
- The control characters represented by simple *escape sequences*, shown in Table 1, for controlling output devices such as terminals or printers

Table 1. The standard escape sequences

Escape sequence	Action on display device	Escape sequence	Action on display device
\a	Alert (beep)	\'	The character '
\b	Backspace	\"	The character "
\f	Form feed	\?	The character ?
\n	Newline	\\	The character \
\r	Carriage return	\o \oo \ooo (o = octal digit)	The character with this octal code

Table 1. The standard escape sequences (continued)

Escape sequence	Action on display device	Escape sequence	Action on display device
\t	Horizontal tab	\xh.. (h..=string of hex digits)	The character with this hexadecimal code
\v	Vertical tab		

Any other characters, depending on the given compiler, can be used in comments, strings, and character constants. These may include the dollar sign or diacriticals, for example. However, the use of such characters may affect portability.

The set of all usable characters is called the *extended character set*, which is always a superset of the basic character set.

Certain languages use characters that require more than one byte. These *multibyte characters* may be included in the extended character set. Furthermore, ANSI C99 provides the integer type wchar_t (*wide character type*), which is large enough to represent any character in the extended character set. The modern *Unicode* character encoding is often used, which extends the standard ASCII code to represent some 35,000 characters from 24 countries.

C99 also introduces *trigraph sequences*. These sequences, shown in Table 2, can be used to input graphic characters that are not available on all keyboards. The sequence ??!, for example, can be entered to represent the "pipe" character |.

Table 2. The trigraph sequences

Trigraph	??=	??(	??/	??)	??'	??<	??!	??>	??-
Meaning	#	[	\	]	^	{			}	~

Identifiers

Identifiers are names of variables, functions, macros, types, etc. Identifiers are subject to the following formative rules:

- An identifier consists of a sequence of letters (A to Z, a to z), digits (0 to 9), and underscores (_).
- The first character of an identifier must not be a digit.
- Identifiers are case-sensitive.
- There is no restriction on the length of an identifier. However, only the first 31 characters are generally significant.

Keywords are reserved and must not be used as identifiers. Following is a list of keywords:

auto	enum	restrict(*)	unsigned
break	extern	return	void
case	float	short	volatile
char	for	signed	while
const	goto	sizeof	_Bool(*)
continue	if	static	_Complex(*)
default	inline(*)	struct	_Imaginary(*)
do	int	switch	
double	long	typedef	
else	register	union	

External names—that is, identifiers of externally linked functions and variables—may be subject to other restrictions, depending on the linker: in portable C programs, external names should be chosen so that only the first eight characters are significant, even if the linker is *not* case-sensitive.

Some examples of identifiers are:

Valid: a, DM, dm, FLOAT, _var1, topOfWindow
Invalid: do, 586_cpu, zähler, nl-flag, US_$

Categories and Scope of Identifiers

Each identifier belongs to exactly one of the following four categories:

- *Label names*
- The *tags* of structures, unions, and enumerations. These are identifiers that follow one of the keywords struct, union, or enum (see "Derived Types").
- Names of structure or union *members*. Each structure or union type has a separate name space for its members.
- All other identifiers, called *ordinary identifiers*.

Identifiers of different categories may be identical. For example, a label name may also be used as a function name. Such re-use occurs most often with structures: the same string can be used to identify a structure type, one of its members, and a variable; for example:

```
struct person {char *person; /*...*/} person;
```

The same names can also be used for members of different structures.

Each identifier in the source code has a *scope*. The scope is that portion of the program in which the identifier can be used. The four possible scopes are:

Function prototype
> Identifiers in the list of parameter declarations of a function prototype (not a function definition) have *function prototype scope*. Because these identifiers have no meaning outside the prototype itself, they are little more than comments.

Function
> Only *label names* have *function scope*. Their use is limited to the function block in which the label is defined. Label names must also be unique within the function. The goto statement causes a jump to a labelled statement within the same function.

Block
> Identifiers declared in a block that are not labels have *block scope*. The parameters in a function definition also have block scope. Block scope begins with the

declaration of the identifier and ends with the closing brace (}) of the block.

File

Identifiers declared outside all blocks and parameter lists have *file scope*. File scope begins with the declaration of the identifier and extends to the end of the source file.

An identifier that is not a label name is not necessarily *visible* throughout its scope. If an identifier with the same category as an existing identifier is declared in a nested block, for example, the outer declaration is temporarily hidden. The outer declaration becomes visible again when the scope of the inner declaration ends.

Basic Types

The *type* of a variable determines how much space it occupies in storage and how the bit pattern stored is interpreted. Similarly, the type of a function determines how its return value is to be interpreted.

Types can be either predefined or derived. The predefined types in C are the *basic types* and the type void. The basic types consist of the *integer types* and the *floating types*.

Integer Types

There are five signed integer types: signed char, short int (or short), int, long int (or long), and long long int(*) (or long long(*)). For each of these types there is a corresponding unsigned integer type with the same storage size. The unsigned type is designated by the prefix unsigned in the type specifier, as in unsigned int.

The types char, signed char, and unsigned char are formally different. Depending on the compiler settings, however, char is equivalent either to signed char or to unsigned char. The prefix signed has no meaning for the types short, int, long, and long long[*], however, since they are always considered to be signed. Thus short and signed short specify the same type.

The storage size of the integer types is not defined; however, their width is ranked in the following order: char <= short <= int <= long <= long long[*]. Furthermore, the size of type short is at least 2 bytes, long at least 4 bytes, and long long at least 8 bytes. Their value ranges for a given implementation are found in the header file *limits.h*.

ANSI C99 also introduces the type _Bool to represent Boolean values. The Boolean value true is represented by 1 and false by 0. If the header file *stdbool.h* has been included, then bool can be used as a synonym for _Bool and the macros true and false for the integer constants 1 and 0. Table 3 shows the standard integer types together with some typical value ranges.

Table 3. Standard integer types with storage sizes and value ranges

Type	Storage size	Value range (decimal)
_Bool	1 byte	0 and 1
char	1 byte	-128 to 127 or 0 to 255
unsigned char	1 byte	0 to 255
signed char	1 byte	-128 to 127
int	2 or 4 bytes	-32,768 to 32,767 or -2,147,483,648 to 2,147,483,647
unsigned int	2 or 4 bytes	0 to 65,535 or 0 to 4,294,967,295
short	2 bytes	-32,768 to 32,767
unsigned short	2 bytes	0 to 65,535
long	4 bytes	-2,147,483,648 to 2,147,483,647
unsigned long	4 bytes	0 to 4,294,967,295
long long[*]	8 bytes	-9,223,372,036,854,775,808 to 9,223,372,036,854,775,807
unsigned long long[*]	8 bytes	0 to 18,446,744,073,709,551,615

ANSI C99 introduced the header file *stdint.h(*)*, which defines integer types with specific widths (see Table 4). The *width N* of an integer type is the number of bits used to represent values of that type, including the sign bit. (Generally, $N = 8, 16, 32$, or 64.)

Table 4. Integer types with defined width

Type	Meaning
int$N$_t	Width is exactly N bits
int_least$N$_t	Width is at least N bits
int_fast$N$_t	The fastest type with width of at least N bits
intmax_t	The widest integer type implemented
intptr_t	Wide enough to store the value of a pointer

For example, `int16_t` is an integer type that is exactly 16 bits wide, and `int_fast32_t` is the fastest integer type that is 32 or more bits wide. These types must be defined for the widths $N = 8, 16, 32$, and 64. Other widths, such as `int24_t`, are optional. For example:

```
int16_t val = -10;   // integer variable
                     // width: exactly 16 bits
```

For each of the signed types described above, there is also an unsigned type with the prefix u. `uintmax_t`, for example, represents the implementation's widest unsigned integer type.

Real and Complex Floating Types

Three types are defined to represent non-integer real numbers: `float`, `double`, and `long double`. These three types are called the *real floating types*.

The storage size and the internal representation of these types are not specified in the C standard, and may vary from one compiler to another. Most compilers follow the IEEE 754-1985 standard for binary floating-point arithmetic, however. Table 5 is also based on the IEEE representation.

Table 5. Real floating types

Type	Storage size	Value range (decimal, unsigned)	Precision (decimal)
float	4 bytes	1.2E-38 to 3.4E+38	6 decimal places
double	8 bytes	2.3E-308 to 1.7E+308	15 decimal places
long double	10 bytes	3.4E-4932 to 1.1E+4932	19 decimal places

The header file *float.h* defines symbolic constants that describe all aspects of the given representation (see "Numerical Limits and Number Classification").

Internal representation of a real floating-point number

The representation of a floating-point number x is always composed of a *sign* s, a *mantissa* m, and an *exponent* exp to base 2:

```
x = s * m * 2exp, where 1.0 <= m < 2  or  m = 0
```

The *precision* of a floating type is determined by the number of bits used to store the mantissa. The *value range* is determined by the number of bits used for the exponent.

Figure 2 shows the storage format for the float type (32-bit) in IEEE representation.

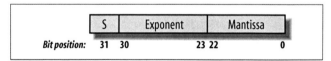

Figure 2. IEEE storage format for the 32-bit float type

The sign bit S has the value 1 for negative numbers and 0 for other numbers. Because in binary the first bit of the mantissa is always 1, it is not represented. The exponent is stored with a bias added, which is 127 for the float type.

For example, the number $-2.5 = -1 * 1.25 * 2^1$ is stored as:

```
S = 1, Exponent = 1+127 = 128, Mantissa = 0.25
```

Complex floating types

ANSI C99 introduces special floating types to represent the complex numbers and the pure imaginary numbers. Every complex number z can be represented in Cartesian coordinates as follows:

```
z = x + i*y
```

where x and y are real numbers and i is the *imaginary unit* $\sqrt{-1}$. The real numbers x and y represent respectively the *real part* and the *imaginary part* of z.

Complex numbers can also be represented in *polar coordinates*:

```
z = r * (cos(theta) + i * sin(theta))
```

The angle theta is called the *argument* and the number r is the *magnitude* or *absolute value* of z.

In C, a complex number is represented as a pair of real and imaginary parts, each of which has type float, double, or long double. The corresponding *complex floating types* are float _Complex, double _Complex, and long double _Complex.

In addition, the *pure imaginary numbers*—i.e., the complex numbers z = i*y where y is a real number—can also be represented by the types float _Imaginary, double _Imaginary, and long double _Imaginary.

Together, the real and the complex floating types make up the *floating types*.

The Type void

The type specifier void indicates that no value is available. It is used in three kinds of situations:

Expressions of type void
> There are two uses for void expressions. First, functions that do not return a value are declared as void. For example:
> ```
> void exit (int status);
> ```

Second, the *cast* construction (void)expression can be used to explicitly discard the value of an expression. For example:

```
(void)printf("An example.");
```

Prototypes of functions that have no parameters
For example:

```
int rand(void);
```

Pointers to void
The type void * (pronounced "pointer to void") represents the address of an object, but not the object's type. Such "typeless" pointers are mainly used in functions that can be called with pointers to different types as parameters. For example:

```
void *memcpy(void *dest, void *source, size_t count);
```

Constants

Every constant is either an *integer constant*, a *floating constant*, a *character constant*, or a *string literal*. There are also *enumeration constants*, which are described in "Enumeration Types." Every constant has a type that is determined by its value and its notation.

Integer Constants

Integer constants can be represented as ordinary decimal numbers, octal numbers, or hexadecimal numbers:

- A *decimal constant* (base 10) begins with a digit that is not 0; for example: 1024

- An *octal constant* (base 8) begins with a 0; for example: 012

- A *hexadecimal constant* (base 16) begins with the two characters 0x or 0X; for example: 0x7f, 0X7f, 0x7F, 0X7F. The hexadecimal digits A to F are not case-sensitive.

The *type* of an integer constant, if not explicitly specified, is the first type in the appropriate hierarchy that can represent its value.

For decimal constants, the hierarchy of types is:

```
int, long, unsigned long, long long(*).
```

For octal or hexadecimal constants, the hierarchy of types is:

```
int, unsigned int, long, unsigned long, long long(*),
unsigned long long(*).
```

Thus, integer constants normally have type int. The type can also be explicitly specified by one of the suffixes L or l (for long), LL(*) or ll(*) (for long long(*)), and/or U or u (for unsigned). Table 6 provides some examples.

Table 6. Examples of integer constants

Decimal	Octal	Hexadecimal	Type
15	017	0xf	int
32767	077777	0x7FFF	int
10U	012U	0xAU	unsigned int
32768U	0100000U	0x8000u	unsigned int
16L	020L	0x10L	long
27UL	033ul	0x1BUL	unsigned long

The macros in Table 7 are defined to represent *constants* of an integer type with a given maximum or minimum width N (e.g., = 8, 16, 32, 64). Each of these macros takes a constant integer as its argument and is replaced by the same value with the appropriate type.

Table 7. Macros for integer constants of minimum or maximum width

Macro	Return type
INTMAX_C()	intmax_t
UINTMAX_C()	uintmax_t
INTN_C()	int_least$N$_t
UINTN_C()	uint_least$N$_t

Floating Constants

A floating constant is represented as a sequence of decimal digits with one decimal point, or an exponent notation. Some examples are:

```
41.9
5.67E-3    // The number  5.67*10-3
```

E can also be written as e. The letter P or p is used to represent a floating constant with an exponent to base 2 (ANSI C99); for example:

```
2.7P+6     // The number  2.7*26
```

The decimal point or the notation of an exponent using E, e, P(*), or p(*) is necessary to distinguish a floating constant from an integer constant.

Unless otherwise specified, a floating constant has type double. The suffix F or f assigns the constant the type float; the suffix L or l assigns it the type long double. Thus the constants in the previous examples have type double, 12.34F has type float, and 12.34L has type long double.

Each of the following constants has type double. All the constants in each row represent the same value:

5.19	0.519E1	0.0519e+2	519E-2
12.	12.0	.12E2	12e0
370000.0	37e+4	3.7E+5	0.37e6
0.000004	4E-6	0.4e-5	.4E-5

Character Constants and String Literals

A *character constant* consists of one or more characters enclosed in single quotes. Some examples are:

```
'0'     'A'     'ab'
```

Character constants have type int. The value of a character constant that contains *one* character is the numerical value of

---

the representation of the character. For example, in the ASCII code, the character constant `'0'` has the value 48, and the constant `'A'` has the value 65.

The value of a character constant that contains more than one character is dependent on the given implementation. To ensure portability, character constants with more than one character should be avoided.

Escape sequences such as `'\n'` may be used in character constants. The characters ' and \ can also be represented this way.

The prefix L can be used to give a character constant the type wchar_t; for example:

```
L'A'    L'\x123'
```

A *string literal* consists of a sequence of characters and escape sequences enclosed in double quotation marks; for example:

```
"I am a string!\n"
```

A string literal is stored internally as an array of char (see "Derived Types") with the string terminator `'\0'`. It is therefore one byte longer than the specified character sequence. The empty string occupies exactly one byte. A string literal is also called a *string constant*, although the memory it occupies may be modified.

The string literal `"Hello!"`, for example, is stored as a char array, as shown in Figure 3.

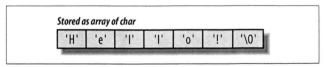

Figure 3. A string literal stored as a char array

String literals that are separated only by whitespace are concatenated into *one* string. For example:

`"hello" " world!"` is equivalent to `"hello world!"`.

Because the *newline* character is also a whitespace character, this concatenation provides a simple way to continue a long string literal in the next line of the source code.

Wide string literals can also be defined as arrays whose elements have type wchar_t. Again, this is done by using the prefix L; for example:

```
L"I am a string of wide characters!"
```

Expressions and Operators

An *expression* is a combination of operators and operands. In the simplest case, an expression consists simply of a constant, a variable, or a function call. Expressions can also serve as operands, and can be joined together by operators into more complex expressions.

Every expression has a type and, if the type is not void, a value. Some examples of expressions follow:

```
4 * 512                         // Type: int
printf("An example!\n")         // Type: int
1.0 + sin(x)                    // Type: double
srand((unsigned)time(NULL))     // Type: void
(int*)malloc(count*sizeof(int)) // Type: int *
```

In expressions with more than one operator, the *precedence* of the operators determines the grouping of operands with operators. The arithmetic operators *, /, and %, for example, take precedence over + and -. In other words, the usual rules apply for the order of operations in arithmetic expressions. For example:

```
4 + 6 * 512    // equivalent to 4 + (6 * 512)
```

If a different grouping is desired, parentheses must be used:

```
(4 + 6) * 512
```

Table 8 lists the precedence of operators.

Table 8. Precedence of operators

Priority	Operator	Grouping
1	`()  []  ->  .`	left to right
2	`!  ~  ++  --  +  -` `(type)  *  &  sizeof`	right to left
3	`*  /  %`	left to right
4	`+  -`	left to right
5	`<<  >>`	left to right
6	`<  <=  >  >=`	left to right
7	`==  !=`	left to right
8	`&`	left to right
9	`^`	left to right
10	`|`	left to right
11	`&&`	left to right
12	`||`	left to right
13	`?:`	right to left
14	`=  +=  -=  *=  /=  %=` `&=  ^=  |=  <<=  >>=`	right to left
15	`,`	left to right

If two operators have equal precedence, then the operands are grouped as indicated in the "Grouping" column of Table 8. For example:

```
2 * 5 / 3     // equivalent to (2 * 5) / 3
```

Operators can be *unary* or *binary*: a unary operator has one operand, while a binary operator has two. This distinction is important for two reasons:

- All unary operators have the same precedence.
- The four characters -, +, *, and & can represent unary or binary operators, depending on the number of operands.

Furthermore, C has one *ternary* operator: the conditional operator ?: has three operands.

The individual operators are briefly described in Tables 9 through 16 in the following sections. The order in which the operands are evaluated is *not* defined, except where indicated. For example, there's no guarantee which of the following functions will be invoked first:

```
f1() + f2() // Which of the two functions is
            // called first is not defined.
```

Arithmetic Operators

Table 9. The arithmetic operators

Operator	Meaning	Example	Result
*	Multiplication	x * y	The product of x and y.
/	Division	x / y	The quotient of x by y.
%	Modulo division	x % y	The remainder of the division x / y.
+	Addition	x + y	The sum of x and y.
-	Subtraction	x - y	The difference of x and y.
+ (unary)	Positive sign	+x	The value of x.
- (unary)	Negative sign	-x	The arithmetic negation of x.
++	Increment	++x x++	x is incremented (x=x+1). The prefixed operator (++x) increments the operand *before* it is evaluated; the postfixed operator (x++) increments the operand *after* it is evaluated.
--	Decrement	--x x--	x is decremented (x=x-1). The prefixed operator (--x) decrements the operand *before* it is evaluated; the postfixed operator (x--) decrements the operand *after* it is evaluated.

The operands of arithmetic operators may have any arithmetic type. Only the % operator requires integer operands.

The *usual arithmetic conversions* may be performed on the operands. For example, 3.0/2 is equivalent to 3.0/2.0. The result has the type of the operands after such conversion.

Note that the result of *division* with integer operands is also an integer! For example:

```
6 / 4       // Result: 1
6 % 4       // Result: 2
6.0 / 4.0   // Result: 1.5
```

The *increment operator* ++ (and analogously, the *decrement operator* --) can be placed either *before* or *after* its operand. A variable x is incremented (i.e., increased by 1) both by ++x (*prefix notation*) and x++ (*postfix notation*). The expressions nonetheless yield different values: the expression ++x has the value of x increased by 1, while the expression x++ yields the prior, unincremented value of x.

Because the operators ++ and -- perform an assignment, their operand must be an lvalue; i.e., an expression that designates a location in memory, such as a variable.

The operators ++, --, + (addition), and – (subtraction) can also be used on pointers. For more information on pointers and pointer arithmetic, see the section "Derived Types."

Assignment Operators

Assignments are performed by *simple* and *compound* assignment operators, as shown in Table 10.

Table 10. Assignment operators

Operator	Meaning	Example	Result
=	Simple assignment	x = y	Assign the value of y to x
op=	Compound assignment	x += y	x op= y is equivalent to x = x op (y) (where op is a binary arithmetic or binary bitwise operator)

The left operand in an assignment must be an lvalue; i.e., an expression that designates an object. This object is assigned a new value.

The simplest examples of lvalues are variable names. In the case of a pointer variable ptr, both ptr and *ptr are lvalues. Constants and expressions such as x+1, on the other hand, are not lvalues.

The following operands are permissible in a *simple assignment* (=):

- Two operands with *arithmetic types*
- Two operands with the same *structure* or *union type*
- Two *pointers* that both point to objects of the *same type*, unless the right operand is the constant NULL

If one operand is a pointer to an object, then the other may be a pointer to the "incomplete" type void (i.e., void *).

If the two operands have different types, the value of the right operand is converted to the type of the left operand.

An *assignment expression* has the type and value of the left operand after the assignment. Assignments are grouped from right to left. For example:

```
a = b = 100;  // equivalent to  a=(b=100);
              // The value 100 is assigned to b and a.
```

A *compound assignment* has the form x op= y, where op is a binary arithmetic operator or a binary bitwise operator. The value of x op (y) is assigned to x. For example:

```
a *= b+1;     // equivalent to  a = a * (b + 1);
```

In a compound assignment x op= y, the expression x is only evaluated once. This is the only difference between x op= y and x = x op (y).

Relational Operators

Every *comparison* is an expression of type int that yields the value 1 or 0. The value 1 means "true" and 0 means "false." Comparisons use the relational operators listed in Table 11.

Table 11. The relational operators

Operator	Meaning	Example	Result: 1 (true) or 0 (false)
<	less than	x < y	1 if x is less than y
<=	less than or equal to	x <= y	1 if x is less than or equal to y
>	greater than	x > y	1 if x is greater than y
>=	greater than or equal to	x >= y	1 if x is greater than or equal to y
==	equal to	x == y	1 if x is equal to y
!=	not equal to	x != y	1 if x is not equal to y. In all other cases, the expression yields 0.

The following operands are permissible for all relational operators:

- Two operands with real arithmetic types. The usual arithmetic conversions may be performed on the operands.
- Two pointers to objects of the same type.

The equality operators == and != can also be used to compare complex numbers. Furthermore, the operands may also be pointers to functions of the same type. A pointer may also be compared with NULL or with a pointer to void. For example:

```
int cmp, *p1, *p2;
. . .
cmp = p1 < p2; // if p1 is less than p2, then cmp = 1;
               // otherwise cmp = 0.
```

Logical Operators

The logical operators, shown in Table 12, can be used to combine the results of several comparison expressions into one logical expression.

Table 12. The logical operators

Operator	Meaning	Example	Result: 1 (true) or 0 (false)
&&	logical AND	x && y	1 if both x and y are not equal to 0

Table 12. The logical operators (continued)

Operator	Meaning	Example	Result: 1 (true) or 0 (false)
||	logical OR	x || y	1 if either or both of x and y is not equal to 0
!	logical NOT	!x	1 if x equals 0. In all other cases, the expression yields 0.

The operands of logical operators may have any scalar (i.e., arithmetic or pointer) type. Any value except 0 is interpreted as "true"; 0 is "false."

Like relational expressions, logical expressions yield the values "true" or "false"; that is, the int values 1 or 0:

```
!x || y  // "(not x) or y" yields 1 (true)
         // if x == 0 or y != 0
```

The operators && and || first evaluate the left operand. If the result of the operation is already known from the value of the left operand (i.e., the left operand of && is 0 or the left operand of || is not 0), then the right operand is not evaluated. For example:

```
i < max  &&  scanf("%d", &x) == 1
```

In this logical expression, the function scanf() is only called if i is less than max.

Bitwise Operators

There are six bitwise operators, described in Table 13. All of them require integer operands.

Table 13. The bitwise operators

Operator	Meaning	Example	Result (for each bit position)
&	bitwise AND	x & y	1, if 1 in both x and y
|	bitwise OR	x | y	1, if 1 in either x or y, or both
^	bitwise exclusive OR	x ^ y	1, if 1 in either x or y, but not both

Table 13. The bitwise operators (continued)

Operator	Meaning	Example	Result (for each bit position)
~	bitwise NOT	~x	1, if 0 in x
<<	shift left	x << y	Each bit in x is shifted y positions to the left
>>	shift right	x >> y	Each bit in x is shifted y positions to the right

The *logical bitwise operators*, & (AND), | (OR), ^ (exclusive OR), and ~ (NOT) interpret their operands bit by bit: a bit that is set, i.e., 1, is considered "true"; a cleared bit, or 0, is "false". Thus, in the result of z = x & y, each bit is set if and only if the corresponding bit is set in both x and y. The usual arithmetic conversions are performed on the operands.

The shift operators << and >> transpose the bit pattern of the left operand by the number of bit positions indicated by the right operand. Integer promotions are performed before-hand on both operands. The result has the type of the left operand after integer promotion. Some examples are:

```
int  x = 0xF, result;
result = x << 4; // yields 0xF0
result = x >> 2; // yields  0x3
```

The bit positions vacated at the right by the left shift << are always filled with 0 bits. Bit values shifted out to the left are lost.

The bit positions vacated at the left by the right shift >> are filled with 0 bits if the left operand is an unsigned type or has a non-negative value. If the left operand is signed and nega-tive, the left bits may be filled with 0 (*logical shift*) or with the value of the sign bit (*arithmetic shift*), depending on the compiler.

Memory Accessing Operators

The operators in Table 14 are used to access objects in mem-ory. The terms used here, such as pointer, array, structure, etc., are introduced later under "Derived Types."

Table 14. Memory accessing operators

Operator	Meaning	Example	Result
&	Address of	&x	A constant pointer to x
*	Indirection	*p	The object (or function) pointed to by p
[ ]	Array element	x[i]	*(x+i), the element with index i in the array x
.	Member of a structure or union	s.x	The member named x in the structure or union s
->	Member of a structure or union	p->x	The member named x in the structure or union pointed to by p

The operand of the *address operator* & must be an expression that designates a function or an object. The address operator & yields the address of its operand. Thus an expression of the form &x is a pointer to x. The operand of & must not be a bit-field, nor a variable declared with the storage class specifier `register`.

The *indirection operator* * is used to access an object or a function through a pointer. If `ptr` is a pointer to an object or function, then `*ptr` designates the object or function pointed to by `ptr`. For example:

```
int  a, *pa;  // An int variable and a pointer to int.

pa  = &a;     // Let pa point to a.
*pa = 123;    // Now equivalent to  a = 123;
```

The *subscript operator* [] can be used to address the elements of an array. If v is an array and i is an integer, then v[i] denotes the element with index i in the array. In more general terms, one of the two operands of the operator [] must be a pointer to an object (e.g., an array name), and the other must be an integer. An expression of the form x[i] is equivalent to (*(x+(i))). For example:

```
float  a[10], *pa; // An array and a pointer.
pa = a;            // Let pa point to a[0].
```

Since pa points to a[0], pa[3] is equivalent to a[3] or *(a+3).

The operators . and -> designate a member of a structure or union. The left operand of the dot operator must have a structure or union type. The left operand of the arrow operator is a pointer to a structure or union. In both cases, the right operand is the name of a member of the type. The result has the type and value of the designated member.

If p is a pointer to a structure or union and x is the name of a member, then p->x is equivalent to (*p).x, and yields the member x of the structure (or union) to which p points.

The operators . and ->, like [], have the highest precedence, so that an expression such as ++p->x is equivalent to ++(p->x).

Other Operators

The operators in Table 15 do not belong to any of the categories described so far.

Table 15. Other operators

Operator	Meaning	Example	Result
()	Function call	pow(x,y)	Execute the function with the arguments x and y
(*type*)	Cast	(long)x	The value of x with the specified type
sizeof	Size in bytes	sizeof(x)	The number of bytes occupied by x
?:	Conditional evaluation	x?y:z	If x is not equal to 0, then y, otherwise z
,	Sequence operator	x,y	Evaluate x first, then y

A *function call* consists of a pointer to a function (such as a function name) followed by parentheses () containing the argument list, which may be empty.

The *cast* operator can only be used on operands with *scalar* types! An expression of the form (*type*)x yields the value of the operand x with the type specified in the parentheses.

The operand of the sizeof operator is either a type name in parentheses or any expression that does not have a function type. The sizeof operator yields the number of bytes required to store an object of the specified type, or the type of the expression. The result is a constant of type size_t.

The *conditional operator* ?: forms a conditional expression. In an expression of the form x?y:z, the left operand x is evaluated first. If the result is not equal to 0 (in other words, if x is "true"), then the second operand y is evaluated, and the expression yields the value of y. However, if x is equal to 0 ("false"), then the third operand z is evaluated, and the expression yields the value of z.

The first operand can have any scalar type. If the second and third operands do not have the same type, then a type conversion is performed. The type to which both can be converted is the type of the result. The following types are permissible for the second and third operands:

- Two operands with arithmetic types.
- Two operands with the same structure or union type, or the type void.
- Two pointers, both of which point to objects of the same type, unless one of them is the constant NULL. If one operand is an object pointer, the other may be a pointer to void.

The *sequence* or *comma operator* , has two operands: first the left operand is evaluated, then the right. The result has the type and value of the right operand. Note that a comma in a list of initializations or arguments is not an operator, but simply a punctuation mark!

Alternative notation for operators

The header file *iso646.h* defines symbolic constants that can be used as synonyms for certain operators, as listed in Table 16.

Table 16. Symbolic constants for operators

Constant	Meaning	Constant	Meaning	Constant	Meaning
and	&&	bitand	&	and_eq	&=
or	||	bitor	|	or_eq	|=
not	!	xor	^	xor_eq	^=
		compl	~	not_eq	!=

Type Conversions

A type conversion yields the value of an expression in a new type. Conversion can be performed only on scalar types, i.e., arithmetic types and pointers.

A type conversion always conserves the original value, if the new type is capable of representing it. Floating-point numbers may be rounded on conversion from double to float, for example.

Type conversions can be *implicit*—i.e., performed by the compiler automatically—or *explicit*, through the use of the *cast operator*. It is considered good programming style to use the cast operator whenever type conversions are necessary. This makes the type conversion explicit, and avoids compiler warnings.

Integer Promotion

Operands of the types _Bool, char, unsigned char, short, and unsigned short, as well as bit-fields, can be used in expressions wherever operands of type int or unsigned int are permissible. In such cases, *integer promotion* is performed on the operands: they are automatically converted to int or unsigned int. Such operands are converted to unsigned int only if the type int cannot represent all values of the original type.

Thus C always "expects" values that have at least type int. If c is a variable of type char, then its value in the expression:

```
c + '0'
```

is promoted to int before the addition takes place.

Usual Arithmetic Conversions

The operands of a binary operator may have different arithmetic types. In this case, the *usual arithmetic conversions* are implicitly performed to cast their values in a common type. However, the usual arithmetic conversions are not performed for the assignment operators, nor for the logical operators && and ||.

If operands still have different types after integer promotion, they are converted to the type that appears highest in the hierarchy shown in Figure 4. The result of the operation also has this type.

When one complex floating type is converted to another, both the type of the real part and the type of the imaginary part are converted according to the rules applicable to the corresponding real floating types.

Type Conversions in Assignments and Pointers

A simple assignment may also involve different arithmetic types. In this case, the value of the right operand is always converted to the type of the left operand.

In a compound assignment, the usual arithmetic conversions are performed for the arithmetic operation. Then any further type conversion takes place as for a simple assignment.

A pointer to void can be converted to any other object pointer. An object pointer can also be converted into a pointer to void. The address it designates—its value—remains unchanged.

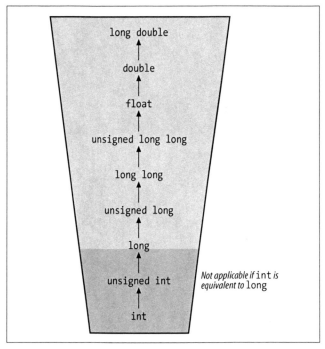

Figure 4. Arithmetic type promotion hierarchy

Statements

A *statement* specifies an action to be performed, such as an arithmetic operation or a function call. Many statements serve to control the flow of a program by defining loops and branches. Statements are processed one after another in sequence, except where such control statements result in jumps.

Every statement that is not a block is terminated by a semicolon.

Block and Expression Statements

A *block*, also called a *compound statement*, groups a number of statements together into one statement. A block can also contain declarations.

The syntax for a block is:

```
{[list of declarations][list of statements]}
```

Here is an example of a block:

```
{ int i = 0;        /* Declarations  */
  static long a;
  extern long max;

  ++a;              /* Statements    */
  if( a >= max)
  {  . . .   }    /* A nested block */
  . . .
}
```

The declarations in a block normally precede the statements. However, ANSI C99 permits free placement of declarations.

New blocks can occur anywhere within a function block. Usually a block is formed wherever the syntax calls for a statement, but the program requires several statements. This is the case, for example, when more than one statement is to be repeated in a loop.

An *expression statement* is an expression followed by a semicolon. The syntax is:

```
[expression] ;
```

Here is an example of an expression statement:

```
y = x;         // Assignment
```

The expression—an assignment or function call, for example—is evaluated for its side effects. The type and value of the expression are discarded.

A statement consisting only of a semicolon is called an *empty statement*, and does not peform any operation. For example:

```
for ( i = 0;  str[i] != '\0'; ++i )
    ;                        // Empty statement
```

Jumps

The following statements can be used to control the program flow:

- Selection statements: if ... else or switch
- Loops: while, do ... while or for
- Unconditional jumps: goto, continue, break or return

---

if ... else

The if statement creates a *conditional jump*.

Syntax: if (*expression*) *statement1* [else *statement2*]

The *expression* must have a scalar type. First, the if statement's controlling expression is evaluated. If the result is not equal to 0—in other words, if the expression yields "true"—then *statement1* is executed. Otherwise, if else is present, *statement2* is executed.

Example:

```
if (x > y)  max = x; // Assign the greater of x and y to
else        max = y; // the variable max.
```

The use of else is optional. If the value of the controlling expression is 0, or "false", and else is omitted, then the program execution continues with the next statement.

If several if statements are nested, then an else clause always belongs to the last if (in the given block nesting level) that does not yet have an else clause. An else can be assigned to a different if by creating explicit blocks.

Example:

```
if ( n > 0 )
{ if ( n % 2 == 0 )
    puts("n is positive and even");
}
else                        // Belongs to first if
    puts("n is negative or zero");
```

---

switch

In a switch statement, the value of the switch expression is compared to the constants associated with case labels. If the expression evaluates to the constant associated with a case label, program execution continues at the matching label. If no matching label is present, program execution branches to the default label if present; otherwise execution continues with the statement following the switch statement.

Syntax: switch (*expression*) *statement*

The *expression* is an integer expression and *statement* is a block statement with case labels and at most one default label. Every case label has the form case *const*:, where *const* is a constant integer expression. All case constants must be different from one another.

Example:

```
switch( command )          // Query a command obtained
{                          // by user input in a menu,
                           // for example.
   case 'a':
   case 'A': action1();    // Carry out action 1,
             break;        // then quit the switch.
   case 'b':
   case 'B': action2();    // Carry out action 2,
             break;        // then quit the switch.
   default:  putchar('\a'); // On any other "command":
                           // alert.
}
```

After the jump from the switch to a label, program execution continues sequentially, regardless of other labels. The break statement can be used to exit the switch block at any time. A break is thus necessary if the statements following other case labels are not to be executed.

Integer promotion is applied to the switch expression. The case constants are then converted to the resulting type of the switch expression.

Loops

A loop consists of a statement or block, called the loop body, that is executed several times, depending on a given condition. C offers three statements to construct loops: while, do ... while, and for.

In each of these loop statements, the number of loop iterations performed is determined by a *controlling expression*. This is an expression of a scalar type, i.e., an arithmetic expression or a pointer. The expression is interpreted as "true" if its value is not equal to 0; otherwise it is considered "false".

Syntactically, the loop body consists of one statement. If several statements are required, they are grouped in a block.

---

while

The while statement is a "top-driven" loop: first the loop condition (i.e., the controlling expression) is evaluated. If it yields "true", the loop body is executed, and then the controlling expression is evaluated again. If it is false, program execution continues with the statement following the loop body.

Syntax: while (*expression*) *statement*

Example:
```
s = str;            // Let the char pointer s
while( *s != '\0') // point to the end of str
    ++s;
```

---

do ... while

The do ... while statement is a "bottom-driven" loop: first the body of the loop is executed, then the controlling expression is evaluated. This is repeated until the controlling expression is "false", or 0.

The key difference from a while statement is that a do ... while loop body is always executed at least once. A while loop may not execute at all, because its expression could be false to begin with.

Syntax: do *statement* while (*expression*) ;

Example:

```
i = 0;
do                          // Copy the string str1
    str2[i] = str1[i];  // to string str2
while ( str1[i++] != '\0' );
```

---

for

A typical for loop uses a control variable and performs the following actions on it:

1. Initialization (once before beginning the loop)
2. Tests the controlling expression
3. Makes adjustments (such as incrementation) at the end of each loop iteration

The three expressions in the head of the for loop define these three actions.

Syntax:

```
for ([expression1]; [expression2]; [expression3])
        statement
```

expression1 and *expression3* can be any expressions. *Expression2* is the controlling expression, and hence must have a scalar type. Any of these expressions can be omitted. If *expression2* is omitted, the loop body is executed unconditionally. In ANSI C99, *expression1* may also be a declaration. The scope of the variable declared is then limited to the for loop.

Example:

```
for (int i = DELAY; i > 0; --i)    // Wait a little
    ;
```

Except for the scope of the variable i, this for loop is equivalent to the following while loop:

```
int i = DELAY; // Initialize
while( i > 0)  // Test the controlling expression
    --i; // Adjust
```

Unconditional Jumps

goto

The goto statement jumps to any point within a function. The destination of the jump is specified by the name of a label.

Syntax: goto *label_name*;

A *label* is a name followed by a colon that appears before any statement.

Example:
```
for ( ... )          // Jump out of
    for ( ... )      // nested loops.
        if ( error )
          goto  handle_error;
  ...
  handle_error:      // Error handling here
  ...
```

The only restriction is that the goto statement and the label must be contained in the same function. Nonetheless, the goto statement should never be used to jump into a block from outside it.

continue

The continue statement can only be used within the body of a loop. It jumps over the remainder of the loop body. Thus in a while or do ... while loop, it jumps to the next test of the controlling expression, and in a for loop it jumps to the evaluation of the per-iteration adjustment expression.

Syntax: continue;

Example:
```
for (i = -10; i < 10; ++i)
{ ...
```

```
    if (i == 0) continue;      // Skip the value 0
    ...
}
```

break

The break statement jumps immediately to the statement after the end of a loop or switch statement. This provides a way to end execution of a loop at any point in the loop body.

Syntax: break;

Example:

```
while (1)
{ ...
  if (command == ESC) break;      // Exit the loop
  ...
}
```

return

The return statement ends the execution of the current function and returns control to the caller. The value of the expression in the return statement is returned to the caller as the *return value* of the function.

Syntax: return *expression*;

Example:

```
int max( int a, int b )      // The maximum of a and b
{ return (a>b ? a : b); }
```

Any number of return statements can appear in a function.

The value of the return expression is converted to the type of the function if necessary.

The expression in the return statement can be omitted. This only makes sense in functions of type void, however—in which case the entire return statement can also be omitted. Then the function returns control to the caller at the end of the function block.

Declarations

A *declaration* determines the interpretation and properties of one or more identifiers. A declaration that allocates storage space for an object or a function is a *definition*. In C, an *object* is a data storage region that contains constant or variable values. The term "object" is thus somewhat more general than the term "variable."

In the source file, declarations can appear at the beginning of a block, such as a function block, or outside of all functions. Declarations that do not allocate storage space, such as function prototypes or type definitions, are normally placed in a header file.

ANSI C99 allows declarations and statements to appear in any order within a block.

General Syntax and Examples

The general syntax of a declaration is as follows:

```
[storage class] type  D1 [, D2, ...];
```

storage class
> One of the storage class specifiers `extern`, `static`, `auto`, or `register`.

type
> A basic type, or one of the following type specifiers: `void`, `enum` *type* (enumeration), `struct` or `union` type, or `typedef` *name*.
>
> *type* may also contain type qualifiers, such as `const`.

D1 [, D2,...]
> A list of declarators. A declarator contains at least one identifier, such as a variable name.

Some examples are:

```
char   letter;
int    i, j, k;
static  double rate, price;
extern char  flag;
```

Variables can be initialized—that is, assigned an initial value—in the declaration. Variable and function declarations are described in detail in the sections that follow.

Complex Declarations

If a declarator contains only one identifier, with or without an initialization, the declaration is called a simple declaration. In a complex declaration, the declarator also contains additional type information. This is necessary in declarations of *pointers*, *arrays*, and *functions*. Such declarations use the three operators, shown in Table 17.

Table 17. Operators for complex declarations

Operator	Meaning
*	Pointer to
[ ]	Array of element type
( )	Function returning value of type

The operators in Table 17 have the same precedence in declarations as in expressions. Parentheses can also be used to group operands.

Complex declarators are always interpreted beginning with the identifier being declared. Then the following steps are repeated until all operators are resolved:

1. Any pair of parentheses () or square brackets [] appearing *to the right* is interpreted.
2. If there are none, then any asterisk appearing *to the left* is interpreted.

For example:

```
char *strptr[100];
```

This declaration identifies strptr as an array. The array's 100 elements are pointers to char.

Variables

Every variable must be declared before it can be used. The declaration determines the variable's *type*, its *storage class*, and possibly its *initial value*. The type of a variable determines how much space it occupies in storage and how the bit pattern it stores is interpreted. For example:

```
float dollars = 2.5F;    // a variable of type float
```

The variable dollars designates a region in memory with a size of 4 bytes. The contents of these four bytes are interpreted as a floating-point number, and initialized with the value 2.5.

Storage Classes

The storage class of a variable determines its *scope*, its *storage duration*, and its *linkage*. The scope can be either *block* or *file* (see "Categories and Scope of Identifiers," earlier in this book). Variables also have one of two storage durations:

Static storage duration
> The variable is generated and initialized once, before the program begins. It exists continuously throughout the execution of the program.

Automatic storage duration
> The variable is generated anew each time the program flow enters the block in which it is defined. When the block is terminated, the memory occupied by the variable is freed.

The storage class of a variable is determined by the position of its declaration in the source file and by the storage class specifier, if any. A declaration may contain no more than one storage class specifier. Table 18 lists the valid storage class specifiers.

Table 18. The storage class specifiers

Specifier	Meaning
auto	Variables declared with the storage class specifier auto have automatic storage duration. The specifier auto is applicable only to variables that are declared within a function. Because the automatic storage class is the default for such variables, the specifier auto is rarely used.
register	The storage class specifier register instructs the compiler to store the variable in a CPU register if possible. As a result, the address operator (&) cannot be used with a register variable. In all other respects, however, register variables are treated the same as auto variables.
static	Variables declared as static always have static storage duration. The storage class specifier static is used to declare static variables with a limited scope.
extern	The specifier extern is used to declare variables with static storage duration that can be used throughout the program.

Table 19 illustrates the possible storage classes and their effect on the scope and the storage duration of variables.

Table 19. Storage class, scope, and storage duration of variables

Position of the declaration	Storage class specifier	Scope	Storage duration
Outside all functions	none, extern, static	File	Static
Within a function	none, auto, register	Block	Automatic
Within a function	extern, static	Block	Static

Initialization

Variables can be *initialized* (assigned an initial value) in their declaration. The initializer consists of an equal sign followed by a constant expression. Some examples are:

```
int index = 0, max = 99, *intptr = NULL;
static char message[20] = "Example!";
```

Variables are not initialized in declarations that do not cause an object to be created, such as function prototypes and declarations that refer to external variable definitions.

Every initialization is subject to the following rules:

1. A variable declaration with an initializer is always a definition. This means that storage is allocated for the variable.

2. A variable with *static storage duration* can only be initialized with a value that can be calculated at the time of compiling. Hence the initial value must be a constant expression.

3. For declarations *without an initializer*: variables with static storage duration are implicitly initialized with NULL (all bytes have the value 0); the initial value of all other variables is undefined!

The type conversion rules for simple assignments are also applied on initialization.

Derived Types

A programmer can also define new types, including *enumerated types* and *derived types*. Derived types include pointers, arrays, structures, and unions.

The basic types and the enumerated types are collectively called the *arithmetic types*. The arithmetic types and the pointer types in turn make up the *scalar types*. The array and structure types are known collectively as the *aggregate types*.

Enumeration Types

Enumeration types are used to define variables that can only be assigned certain discrete integer values throughout the program. The possible values and names for them are defined in an enumeration. The type specifier begins with the keyword enum; for example:

```
enum toggle { OFF, ON, NO = 0, YES };
```

The list of enumerators inside the braces defines the new enumeration type. The identifier `toggle` is the *tag* of this enumeration. This enumeration defines the identifiers in the list (OFF, ON, NO, and YES) as constants with type int.

The value of each identifier in the list may be determined explicitly, as in `NO = 0` in the example above. Identifiers for which no explicit value is specified are assigned a value automatically based on their position in the list, as follows: An enumerator without an explicit value has the value 0 if it is the first in the list; otherwise its value is 1 greater than that of the preceding enumerator. Thus in the example above, the constants OFF and NO have the value 0, while ON and YES have the value 1.

Once an enumeration type has been defined, variables with the type can be declared within its scope. For example:

```
enum toggle t1, t2 = ON;
```

This declaration defines t1 and t2 as variables with type enum toggle, and also initializes t2 with the value ON, or 1.

Following is an enumeration without a tag:

```
enum { black, blue, green, cyan, red, magenta, white };
```

As this example illustrates, the definition of an enumeration does not necessarily include a *tag*. In this case, the enumeration type cannot be used to declare variables, but the enumeration constants can be used to designate a set of discrete values. This technique can be used as an alternative to the #define directive. The constants in the example above have the following values: black = 0, blue = 1, ... , white = 6.

Variables with an enumeration type can generally be used in a C program—in comparative or arithmetic expressions, for example—as ordinary int variables.

Structures, Unions, and Bit-Fields

Different data items that make up a logical unit are generally grouped together in a record. The structure of a record—i.e., the names, types, and order of its components—is represented in C by a *structure type*.

The components of a record are called the *members* of the structure. Each member can be of any type. The type specifier begins with the keyword struct; for example:

```
struct article    {    char   name[40];
                       int    quantity;
                       double price;
                  };
```

This example declares a structure type with three members. The identifier article is the tag of the structure, and name, quantity, and price are the names of its members. Within the scope of a structure declaration, variables can be declared with the structure type:

```
struct article  a1, a2, *pArticle, arrArticle[100];
```

a1 and a2 are variables of type struct article, and pArticle is a pointer to an object of type struct article. The array arrArticle has 100 elements of type struct article.

Structure variables can also be declared simultaneously with the structure type definition. If no further reference is made to a structure type, then its declaration need not include a tag. For example:

```
struct {unsigned char character, attribute;}
xchar, xstr[100];
```

The structure type defined here has the members character and attribute, both of which have the type unsigned char. The variable xchar and the elements of the array xstr have the type of the new tagless structure.

The members of a structure variable are located in memory in order of their declaration within the structure. The address of the first member is identical to the address of the entire structure. The addresses of the other members and the total storage space required by the structure may vary, however, since the compiler can insert unnamed gaps between the individual members for the sake of optimization. For this reason the storage size of a structure should always be obtained using the sizeof operator.

The macro offsetof, defined in the header file *stddef.h*, can be used to obtain the location of a member within a structure. The expression:

```
offsetof( structure_type, member )
```

has the type size_t, and yields the distance in bytes between the beginning of the structure and member.

Structure variables can be *initialized* by an initialization list containing a value for each member:

```
struct article flower =     // Declare and initialize the
    { "rose", 7, 2.49 };    // structure variable flower
```

A structure variable with automatic storage duration can also be initialized with the value of an existing structure variable. The assignment operator can be used on variables of the same structure type. For example:

```
arrArticle[0] = flower;
```

This operation copies the value of each member of flower to the corresponding member of arrArticle[0].

A specific structure member can be *accessed* by means of the dot operator, which has a structure variable and the name of a member as its operands:

```
flower.name     // The array 'name'
flower.price    // The double variable 'price'
```

Efficient data handling often requires the use of *pointers to structures*. The arrow operator provides convenient access to a member of a structure identified by a pointer. The left operand of the arrow operator is a pointer to a structure. Some examples follow:

```
pArticle = &flower;      // Let pArticle point to flower
pArticle->quantity       // Access members of flower
pArticle->price          // using the pointer pArticle
```

A structure cannot have itself as a member. *Recursive structures* can be defined, however, by means of members that are pointers to the structure's own type. Such recursive structures are used to implement linked lists and binary trees, for example.

Unions

A *union* permits references to the same location in memory to have different types. The declaration of a union differs from that of a structure only in the keyword union:

```
union number {long n; double x;};
```

This declaration creates a new union type with the tag number and the two members n and x.

Unlike the members of a structure, all the members of a union begin at the same address! Hence the size of a union is that of its largest member. According to the example above, a variable of type union number occupies 8 bytes.

Once a union type has been defined, variables of that type can be declared. Thus:

```
union number  nx[10];
```

declares an array nx with ten elements of type union number. At any given time, each such element contains either a long or a double value. The members of a union can be accessed in the same ways as structure members. For example:

```
nx[0].x = 1.234;    // Assign a double value to nx[0]
```

Like structures, union variables are *initialized* by an initializer list. For a union, however, the list contains only one initializer. If no union member is explicitly designated, the

---

first member named in the union type declaration is initialized:

```
union number length = { 100L };
```

After this declaration, length.n has the value 100.

Bit-fields

Members of structures or unions can also be *bit-fields*. Bit-fields are integers which consist of a defined number of bits. The declaration of a bit-field has the form:

```
type    [identifier] : width;
```

where *type* is either unsigned int or signed int, *identifier* is the optional name of the bit-field, and *width* is the number of bits occupied by the bit-field in memory.

A bit-field is normally stored in a machine word that is a storage unit of length sizeof(int). The width of a bit-field cannot be greater than that of a machine word. If a smaller bit-field leaves sufficient room, subsequent bit-fields may be packed into the same storage unit. A bit-field with width zero is a special case, and indicates that the subsequent bit-field is to be stored in a new storage unit regardless of whether there's room in the current storage unit. Here's an example of a structure made up of bit fields:

```
struct    {    unsigned int  b0_2 : 3;
               signed   int  b3_7 : 5;
               unsigned int       : 7;
               unsigned int  b15  : 1;
          } var;
```

The structure variable var occupies at least two bytes, or 16 bits. It is divided into four bit-fields: var.b0_2 occupies the lowest three bits, var.b3_7 occupies the next five bits, and var.b15 occupies the highest bit. The third member has no name, and only serves to define a gap of seven bits, as shown in Figure 5.

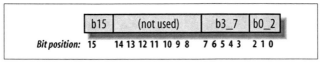

Bit position: 15   14 13 12 11 10 9 8   7 6 5 4 3 2 1 0

Figure 5. Bit assignments in the example struct

Bit-fields with the type unsigned int are interpreted as unsigned. Bit-fields of type signed int can have negative values in two's-complement encoding. In the example above, var.b0_2 can hold values in the range from 0 to 7, and var.b3_7 can take values in the range from −16 to 15.

Bit-fields also differ from ordinary integer variables in the following ways:

- The address operator (&) cannot be applied to bit-fields (but it can be applied to a structure variable that contains bit-fields).
- Some uses of bit-fields may lead to portability problems, since the interpretation of the bits within a word can differ from one machine to another.

Arrays

Arrays are used to manage large numbers of objects of the same type. Arrays in C can have elements of any type except a function type. The definition of an array specifies the *array name*, the *type*, and, optionally, the *number* of array elements. For example:

```
char line[81];
```

The array line consists of 81 elements with the type char. The variable line itself has the derived type "array of char" (or "char array").

In a statically defined array, the number of array elements (i.e., the *length* of the array) must be a constant expression. In ANSI C99, any integer expression with a positive value can be used to specify the length of a non-static array with block scope. This is also referred to as a *variable-length array*.

An array always occupies a *continuous* location in memory. The size of an array is thus the number of elements times the size of the element type:

```
sizeof( line ) == 81 * sizeof( char ) == 81 bytes
```

The individual array elements can be accessed using an index. In C, the first element of an array has the index 0. Thus the 81 elements of the array line are line[0], line[1], ... , line[80].

Any integer expression can be used as an index. It is up to the programmer to ensure that the value of the index lies within the valid range for the given array.

A *string* is a sequence of consecutive elements of type char that ends with the null character, '\0'. The length of the string is the number of characters excluding the string terminator '\0'. A string is stored in a char array, which must be at least one byte longer than the string.

A *wide string* consists of characters of type wchar_t and is terminated by the wide null character, L'\0'. The *length* of a wide string is the number of wchar_t characters in the string, excluding the wide string terminator. For example:

```
wchar_t wstr[20] = L"Mister Fang"; // length: 11
                                   // wide characters
```

A *multi-dimensional array* in C is an array whose elements are themselves arrays. For example:

```
short point[50][20][10];
```

The three-dimensional array point consists of 50 elements that are two-dimensional arrays. The declaration above defines a total of 50*20*10 = 10,000 elements of type short, each of which is uniquely identified by three indices:

```
point[0][0][9] = 7; // Assign the value 7 to  the "point"
                    // with the "coordinates" (0,0,9).
```

Two-dimensional arrays, also called *matrices*, are the most common multi-dimensional arrays. The elements of a matrix can be thought of as being arranged in rows (first index) and columns (second index).

Arrays in C are closely related to *pointers*: in almost all expressions, the name of an array is converted to a pointer to the first element of the array. The `sizeof` operator is an exception, however: if its operand is an array, it yields the number of bytes occupied, not by a pointer, but by the array itself. After the declaration:

```
char msg[] = "Hello, world!";
```

the array name msg points to the character 'H'. In other words, msg is equivalent to &msg[0]. Thus in a statement such as:

```
puts( msg ); // Print string to display
```

only the address of the beginning of the string is passed to the function `puts()`. Internally, the function processes the characters in the string until it encounters the terminator character '\0'.

An array is *initialized* by an initialization list containing a constant initial value for each of the individual array elements:

```
double x[3] = { 0.0, 0.5, 1.0 };
```

After this definition, x[0] has the value 0.0, x[1] the value 0.5, and x[2] the value 1.0. If the length of the array is greater than the number of values in the list, then all remaining array elements are initialized with 0. If the initialization list is longer than the array, the redundant values are ignored.

The length of the array need not be explicitly specified, however:

```
double x[] = { 0.0, 0.5, 1.0 };
```

In this definition, the length of the array is determined by the number of values in the initialization list.

A char array can be initialized by a string literal:

```
char str[] = "abc";
```

This definition allocates and initializes an array of four bytes, and is equivalent to:

```
char str[] = { 'a', 'b', 'c', '\0' } ;
```

In the *initialization of a multi-dimensional array*, the magnitude of all dimensions except the first must be specified. In the case of a two-dimensional array, for example, the number of rows can be omitted. For example:

```
char error_msg[][40] =    { "Error opening file!",
                            "Error reading file!",
                            "Error writing to file!"};
```

The array error_msg consists of three rows, each of which contains a string.

Pointers

A pointer represents the *address* and *type* of a variable or a function. In other words, for a variable x, &x is a pointer to x.

A pointer refers to a location in memory, and its type indicates how the data at this location is to be interpreted. Thus the pointer types are called pointer to char, pointer to int, and so on, or for short, char pointer, int pointer, etc.

Array names and expressions such as &x are *address constants* or *constant pointers*, and cannot be changed. Pointer variables, on the other hand, store the address of the object to which they refer, which address you may change. A pointer variable is declared by an asterisk (*) prefixed to the identifier. For example:

```
float  x, y, *pFloat;
pFloat = &x;     // Let pFloat point to x.
```

After this declaration, x and y are variables of type float, and pFloat is a variable of type float * (pronounced "pointer to float"). After the assignment operation, the value of pFloat is the address of x.

The *indirection operator* * is used to access data by means of pointers. If ptr is a pointer, for example, then *ptr is the object to which ptr points. For example:

```
y = *pFloat;   // equivalent to  y = x;
```

As long as pFloat points to x, the expression *pFloat can be used in place of the variable x. Of course, the indirection operator * must only be used with a pointer which contains a valid address.

A pointer with the value 0 is called a *null pointer*. Null pointers have a special significance in C. Because all objects and functions have non-zero addresses, a null pointer always represents an invalid address. Functions that return a pointer can therefore return a null pointer to indicate a failure condition. The constant NULL is defined in *stdio.h*, *stddef.h*, and other header files as a null pointer (i.e., a pointer with a value of zero).

All object pointer variables have the same storage size, regardless of their type. Two or four bytes are usually required to store an address.

Parentheses are sometimes necessary in complex pointer declarations. For example:

```
long arr[10];       // Array arr with ten elements
long (*pArr)[10];   // Pointer pArr to an array
                    //  of ten long elements
```

Without the parentheses, the declaration long *pArr[10]; would create an array of ten pointers to long. Parentheses are always necessary in order to declare pointers to arrays or functions.

Pointer arithmetic

Two *arithmetic operations* can be performed on pointers:

- An integer can be added to or subtracted from a pointer.
- One pointer can be subtracted from another of the same type.

These operations are generally useful only when the pointers point to elements of the same array. In arithmetic operations on pointers, the size of the objects pointed to is automatically taken into account. For example:

```
int a[3] = { 0, 10, 20 };  // An array with three elements
int *pa = a;               // Let pa point to a[0]
```

Since pa points to a[0], the expression pa + 1 yields a pointer to the next array element, a[1], which is sizeof(int) bytes away in memory. Furthermore, because the array name a likewise points to a[0], a+1 also yields a pointer to a[1].

Thus for any integer i, the following expressions are equivalent:

```
&a[i] , a+i , pa+i // pointers to the i-th array element
```

By the same token, the following expressions are also equivalent:

```
a[i] , *(a+i) , *(pa+i) , pa[i]  // the i-th array element
```

Thus a pointer can be treated as an array name: pa[i] and *(pa+i) are equivalent. Unlike the array name, however, pa is a variable, not an address constant. For example:

```
pa = a+2;      // Let pa point to a[2]
int n = pa-a;  //  n = 2
```

The subtraction of two pointers yields the number of array elements between the pointers. For example, the expression pa-a yields the integer value 2 if pa points to a[2]. This value has the integer type ptrdiff_t, which is defined (usually as int) in *stddef.h*.

The addition of two pointers is not a useful operation, and hence is not permitted. It is possible, however, to *compare* two pointers of the same type, as the following example illustrates:

```
// Formatted output of the elements of an array
#define  LEN  10
float numbers[LEN], *pn;
    . . .
```

```
for ( pn = numbers; pn < numbers+LEN; ++pn )
    printf( "%16.4f", *pn );
```

Function pointers

The name of a function is a constant pointer to the function. Its value is the address of the function's machine code in memory. For example, the name puts is a pointer to the function puts(), which outputs a string:

```
#include <stdio.h>          // Include declaration of puts()
int (*pFunc)(const char*);  // Pointer to a function
    . . .                   // whose parameter is a string
                            // and whose return value
                            // has type int
pFunc = puts;               // Let pFunc point to puts()
(*pFunc)("Any questions?"); // Call puts() using the
                            // pointer
```

Note that the first pair of parentheses is required in the declaration of the variable pFunc. Without it, int *pFunc(const char*); would declare pFunc as a function that returns a pointer to int.

Type Qualifiers and Type Definitions

The type of an object can be qualified by the keywords const and volatile in the declaration.

The type qualifier const indicates that the program can no longer modify an object after its declaration. For example:

```
const double pi = 3.1415927;
```

After this declaration, a statement that modifies the object pi, such as pi = pi+1;, is illegal and results in a compiler error.

The type qualifier volatile indicates variables that can be modified by processes other than the present program. Based on this information, the compiler may refrain from optimizing access to the variable.

The type qualifiers volatile and const can also be combined:

```
extern const volatile unsigned  clock_ticks;
```

After this declaration, clock_ticks cannot be modified by the program, but may be modified by another process, such as a hardware clock interrupt handler.

Type qualifiers are generally prefixed to the type specifier. In pointer declarations, however, type qualifiers may be applied both to the pointer itself and to the object it addresses. If the type qualifier is to be applied to the pointer itself, it must be placed immediately before the identifier.

The most common example of such a declaration is the "pointer to a constant object." Such a pointer may point to a variable, but cannot be used to modify it. For this reason, such pointers are also called "read-only" pointers. For example:

```
int var1 = 1, var2 = 2, *ptr;
const int cArr[2];
const int *ptrToConst;// "Read-only pointer" to int
```

The following statements are now permitted:

```
ptrToConst = &cArr[0];    // Change the value of
++ptrToConst;             // the pointer variable
ptrToConst = &var1;
var2 = *ptrToConst;       // "Read" access
```

The following statements are *not* permitted:

```
ptr = ptrToConst;    // "Read-only" cannot be copied to
                     // "read-write"
*ptrToConst = 5;     // "Write" access not allowed!
```

restrict

ANSI C99 introduces the type qualifier restrict, which is only applicable to pointers. If a pointer declared with the restrict qualifier points to an object that is to be modified, then the object can only be accessed using that pointer. This information allows the compiler to generate optimized machine code. It is up to the programmer to ensure that the restriction is respected!

Example:

```
void *memcpy( void * restrict dest,     // destination
              const void* restrict src, // source
              size_t n );
```

In using the standard function memcpy() to copy a memory block of n bytes, the programmer must ensure that the source and destination blocks do not overlap.

---

typedef

The keyword typedef is used to give a type a new name.

Examples:

```
typedef unsigned char UCHAR;
typedef struct { double x, y } POINT;
```

After these type definitions, the identifier UCHAR can be used as an abbreviation for the type unsigned char, and the identifier POINT can be used to specify the given structure type.

Examples:

```
UCHAR  c1, c2, tab[100];
POINT point, *pPoint;
```

In a typedef declaration, the identifier is declared as the new type name. The same declaration without the typedef keyword would declare a variable and not a type name.

Functions

Every C program contains at least the function main(), which is the first function executed when the program starts. All other functions are subroutines.

The definition of a function lists the statements it executes. Before a function can be called in a given translation unit, it must be declared. A function definition also serves as a declaration of the function. The declaration of a function informs the compiler of its return type. For example:

```
extern double pow();
```

Here pow() is declared as a function that returns a value with type double. Because function names are external names by default, the storage class specifier extern can also be omitted.

In ANSI C99, implicit function declarations are no longer permitted. Formerly, calls to undeclared functions were allowed, and the compiler implicitly assumed in such cases that the function returned a value of type int.

The declaration of the function pow() in the example above contains no information about the number and type of the function's parameters. Hence the compiler has no way of testing whether the arguments supplied in a given function call are compatible with the function's parameters. This missing information is supplied by a function prototype.

Function Prototypes

A function prototype is a declaration that indicates the types of the function's parameters as well as its return value. For example:

```
double pow( double, double );    // prototype of pow()
```

This prototype informs the compiler that the function pow() expects two arguments of type double, and returns a result of type double. Each parameter type may be followed by a parameter name. This name has no more significance than a comment, however, since its scope is limited to the function prototype itself. For example:

```
double pow( double base, double exponent );
```

Functions that do not return any result are declared with the type specifier void. For example:

```
void func1( char *str ); // func1 expects one string
                         // argument and has no return
                         // value.
```

Functions with no parameters are declared with the type specifier void in the parameter list:

```
int  func2( void );      // func2 takes no arguments and
                         // returns a value with type int.
```

Function declarations should always be in prototype form.
All standard C functions are declared in one (or more) of the
standard header files. For example, *math.h* contains the prototypes of the mathematical functions, such as sin(), cos(),
pow(), etc., while *stdio.h* contains the prototypes of the standard input and output functions.

Function Definitions

The general form of a function definition is:

```
[storage_class] [type] name(
[parameter_list] ) // function declarator
{
    /* declarations, statements */       // function body
}
```

storage_class
> One of the storage class specifiers extern or static.
> Because extern is the default storage class for functions,
> most function definitions do not include a storage class
> specifier.

type
> The type of the function's return value. This can be
> either void or any other type, except an array.

name
> The name of the function.

parameter_list
> The declarations of the function's parameters. If the
> function has no parameters, the list is empty.

Here is one example of a function definition:

```
long sum( int arr[], int len )// Find the sum of the first
{                             // len elements of the array arr
   int i;
   long result = 0;
```

```
    for( i = 0;   i < len;   ++i )
       result += (long)arr[i];
    return result;
}
```

Because by default *function names* are external names, the functions of a program can be distributed among different source files, and can appear in any sequence within a source file.

Functions that are declared as `static`, however, can only be called using their name in the same translation unit in which they are defined. But it is not possible to define functions with block scope—in other words, a function definition cannot appear within another function.

The *parameters* of a function are ordinary variables whose scope is limited to the function. When the function is called, they are initialized with the values of the arguments received from the caller.

The *statements in the function body* define what the function does. When the flow of execution reaches a `return` statement or the end of the function body, control returns to the calling function.

A function that calls itself, directly or indirectly, is called *recursive*. C permits the definition of recursive functions, since variables with automatic storage class are created anew—generally in stack memory—with each function call.

The function declarator shown above is in *prototype style*. Today's compilers still support the older *Kernighan-Ritchie style*, however, in which the parameter identifiers and the parameter type declarations are separate. For example:

```
long sum( arr, len )    // Parameter identifier list
int arr[], len;         // Parameter declarations
{ ... }                 // Function body
```

In ANSI C99, functions can also be defined as *inline*. The `inline` function specifier instructs the compiler to optimize the speed of the function call, generally by inserting the function's machine code directly into the calling routine. The `inline` keyword is prefixed to the definition of the function:

```
inline int max( int x, int y )
{ return ( x >= y ? x : y ); }
```

If an inline function contains too many statements, the compiler may ignore the `inline` specifier and generate a normal function call.

An inline function must be defined in the same translation unit in which it is called. In other words, the function body must be visible when the inline "call" is compiled. It is therefore a good idea to define inline functions—unlike ordinary functions—in a header file.

Inline functions are an alternative to macros with parameters. In translating a macro, the preprocessor simply substitutes text. An inline function, however, behaves like a normal function—so that the compiler tests for compatible arguments, for example—but without the jump to and from another code location.

Function Calls

A function call is an expression whose value and type are those of the function's return value.

The number and the type of the arguments in a function call must agree with the number and type of the parameters in the function definition. Any expression, including constants and arithmetic expressions, may be specified as an argument in a function call. When the function is called, the *value* of the argument is *copied* to the corresponding parameter of the function! For example:

```
double x=0.5, y, pow();    // Declaration
y = pow( 1.0 + x, 2.5 );   // Call to pow() yields
                           // the double value (1.0+x)^2.5
```

In other words, the arguments are passed to the function *by value*. The function itself cannot modify the values of the arguments in the calling function: it can only access its local copy of the values.

In order for a function to modify the value of a variable directly, the caller must give the function the *address* of the variable as an argument. In other words, the variable must be passed to the function *by reference*. Examples of functions that accept arguments by reference include scanf(), time(), and all functions that have an array as one of their parameters. For example:

```
double swap( double *px, double *py ) // Exchange values
                                       // of two variables
{ double z = *px; *px = *py; *py = z; }
```

The arguments of a function are subject to implicit type conversion:

- If the function was declared in prototype form (as is usually the case), each argument is converted to the type of the corresponding parameter, as for an assignment.

- If no prototype is present, *integer promotion* is performed on each integer argument. Arguments of type float are converted to double.

Functions with Variable Numbers of Arguments

Functions that can be called with a variable number of arguments always expect a fixed number of *mandatory* arguments—at least one is required—and a variable number of *optional* arguments. A well-known example is the function printf(): the format string argument is mandatory, while all other arguments are optional. Internally, printf() determines the number and type of the other arguments from the information in the format string.

In the function declarator, optional arguments are indicated by three dots (...). For example:

```
int printf( char *str, ... );      // Prototype
```

In the function definition, the optional arguments are accessed through an object with the type va_list, which contains the argument information. This type is defined in the header file *stdarg.h*, along with the macros va_start, va_arg, and va_end, which are used to manage the arguments.

In order to read the optional arguments, the function must carry out the following steps:

1. Declare an object of type va_list. In the following example, this object is named arglist.

2. Invoke the macro va_start to prepare the arglist object to return the first optional argument. The parameters of va_start are the arglist object and the name of the last mandatory parameter.

3. Invoke the macro va_arg with the initialized arglist object to obtain each of the optional arguments in sequence. The second parameter of va_arg is the type of the optional argument that is being obtained.

   After each invocation of the va_arg macro, the arglist object is prepared to deliver the first optional argument that has not yet been read. The result of va_arg has the type specified by the second argument.

4. After reading out the argument list, the function should invoke the va_end macro before returning control to the caller. The only parameter of va_end is the arglist object.

Following is an example of a function, named max, that accepts a variable number of arguments:

```c
// Determine the maximum of a number of positive integers.
// Parameters: a variable number of positive values of
// type unsigned int. The last argument must be 0.
// Return value: the maximum of the arguments

#include <stdarg.h>
unsigned int max( unsigned int first, ... )
{
    unsigned int maxarg, arg;
```

```
        va_list arglist;   // The optional-argument
                           // list object
        va_start( arglist, first ); // Set arglist to deliver
                                    // the first optional
                                    // argument
    arg = maxarg = first;
    while ( arg != 0 )
    { arg = va_arg( arglist, unsigned );// Get an argument
      if ( arg > maxarg )  maxarg = arg;
    }
    va_end( arglist );         // Finished reading the
                               // optional arguments
    return maxarg;
}
```

Linkage of Identifiers

An identifier that is declared more than once, whether in different scopes (in different files, for example) or in the same
scope, may refer to the same variable or function. Identifiers
must be "linked" in this way in order for a variable to be
used "globally," across different source files, for example.

Each identifier has either *external*, *internal*, or *no* linkage.
These three kinds of linkage have the following significance:

External linkage

An identifier with *external linkage* represents the same
object or function throughout the entire program, i.e., in
all source files and libraries belonging to the program.
The identifier is made known to the linker.

When a second declaration of the same identifier with
external linkage occurs, the linker associates the identifier with the same object or function. A declaration of an
existing external object is sometimes called a *reference
declaration*.

Internal linkage

An identifier with *internal linkage* represents the same
object or function within a given translation unit. The
linker has no information about identifiers with internal

linkage. Thus they remain "internal" to the translation unit.

No linkage

If an identifier has no linkage, then any further declaration using the identifier declares something new, such as a new variable or a new type.

The linkage of an identifier is determined by its storage class; that is, by the position of the declaration and any storage class specifier included in it. Only identifiers of variables and functions can have internal or external linkage. All other identifiers, and identifiers of variables with automatic storage class, have no linkage. Table 20 summarizes this information.

Table 20. Linkage of identifiers

Linkage	Identifiers with this linkage
External	Names of variables either declared with the storage class specifier `extern`, or declared outside of all functions and without a storage class specifier. Names of functions defined without the specifier `static`.
Internal	Names of functions and variables declared outside of all functions and with the specifier `static`.
None	All other identifiers, such as function parameters.

The form of *external names* (identifiers with external linkage) is subject to restrictions, depending on the linker implementation: some linkers only recognize the first eight characters of a name, and do not distinguish between upper- and lower-case letters.

Preprocessing Directives

The C compiler preprocesses every source file before performing the actual translation. The preprocessor removes comments and replaces macros with their definitions.

Every preprocessing directive appears on a line by itself, beginning with the character #. If the directive is long, it can be continued on the next line by inserting a backslash (\) as the last character before the line break.

#define

The #define directive is used to define macros.

Syntax:

```
#define name[(parameter_list)]  [replacement_text]
```

The preprocessor replaces each occurrence of *name* or *name(parameter_list)* in the subsequent source code with *replacement_text*.

Examples:

```
#define  BUF_SIZE  512         // Symbolic constant
#define  MAX(a,b)  ((a) > (b) ? (a) : (b))
```

These directives define the macros BUF_SIZE and MAX. If the replacement text is a constant expression, the macro is also called a *symbolic constant*. Macros can also be nested; a macro, once defined, can be used in another macro definition.

In the previous example, the parentheses are necessary in order for the substitution to be performed correctly when MAX is used in an expression, or when complex expressions replace the parameters a and b. For example, the preprocessor replaces the macro invocation:

```
result = 2 * MAX( x, y & 0xFF );
```

with:

```
result = 2 * ( (x) > (y & 0xFF) ? (x) : (y & 0xFF) );
```

The # Operator

In the macro replacement text, the parameters of the macro may be preceded by the operator # (called the hash or string-izing operator). In this case, the preprocessor sets the corresponding argument in quotation marks, thus converting it into a string.

Example:

```
#define print_int(i) printf( "value " #i " = %d", i )
```

If x and y are variables with type int, then the statement:

```
print_int(x-y);
```

is replaced with:

```
printf( "value ""x-y"" = %d", x-y );
```

Because consecutive string literals are concatenated, this is equivalent to:

```
printf( "value x-y = %d", x-y );
```

The ## Operator

If a macro parameter appears in the replacement text preceded or followed by the operator ## (called the *double-hash* or *token-pasting* operator), then the preprocessor concatenates the tokens to the left and right of the operator, ignoring any spaces. If the resulting text also contains a macro name, then macro replacement is performed once again.

Example:

```
#define show( var, num )  \
        printf( #var #num " = %.1f\n", var ## num )
```

If the float variable x5 has the value 16.4, then the macro invocation:

```
show( x, 5 );
```

is replaced with:

```
printf( "x" "5" " = %.1f\n", x5 );
// Output: x5 = 16.4\n
```

#undef

The #undef directive cancels a macro definition. This is necessary when the definition of a macro needs to be changed, or when a function of the same name needs to be called.

Syntax: #undef *name*

No parameter list needs to be specified, even if the previously defined macro has parameters.

Example:

```
#include <ctype.h>
#undef  toupper
   . . .
c = toupper(c);  // Call the function toupper()
```

#include

The #include directive instructs the preprocessor to insert the contents of a specified file in the program at the point where the #include directive appears.

Syntax:

```
#include   <filename>
#include   "filename"
```

If the filename is enclosed in angle brackets, the preprocessor only searches for it in certain directories. These directories are usually named in the environment variable INCLUDE.

If the filename is enclosed in quotation marks, the preprocessor first looks for the file in the current working directory.

The *filename* may contain a directory path. In this case, the file is only looked for in the specified directory.

The files named in include directives are generally "header" files containing declarations and macro definitions for use in several source files, and have names ending in *.h*. Such files may in turn contain further #include directives.

In the following example, one file to be included is selected based on the value of a symbolic constant:

```
#include <stdio.h>
#include "project.h"

#if VERSION == 1
  #define  MYPROJ_H   "version1.h"
#else
  #define  MYPROJ_H   "version2.h"
#endif

#include MYPROJ_H
```

#if, #elif, #else, #endif

These directives are used to present source code to the compiler only on certain conditions. In this way a different selection of program statements can be compiled from one build to another. This technique can be used to adapt a single program to a variety of target systems, for example, without requiring modification of the source code.

Syntax:

```
#if expression1
  [text1]
[#elif  expression2
  text2]

   . . .
[#elif  expression(n)
  text(n)]
[#else
  text(n+1)]
  #endif
```

Each #if directive may be followed by any number of #elif directives, and at most one #else directive. The conditional source code section must be closed by an #endif directive.

The preprocessor evaluates *expression1*, *expression2*, etc. in succession. At the first expression whose value is "true", i.e., not equal to 0, the conditional code is processed. If none of the expressions is true, then the #else directive is processed, if present.

expression1, *expression2*, etc. must be constant integer expressions. The cast operator cannot be used in preprocessing directives.

The conditional text consists of program code, including other preprocessing directives and ordinary C statements. Conditional text that the preprocessor skips over is effectively removed from the program.

The defined operator

The defined operator can be used to verify whether a given macro name is currently defined.

Syntax: defined (*name*)

The operator yields a non-zero value if a valid definition exists for *name*; otherwise it yields the value 0. A macro name defined by a #define directive remains defined until it is cancelled by an #undef directive. A macro name is considered to be defined even if no replacement text is specified after *name* in the #define directive.

The defined operator is typically used in #if and #elif directives:

```
#if defined(VERSION)
...
#endif
```

Unlike the #ifdef and #ifndef directives, the defined operator yields a value that can be used in a preprocessor expression:

```
#if defined(VERSION) && defined(STATUS)
...
#endif
```

#ifdef and #ifndef

The #ifdef and #ifndef directives can be used to make program text directly conditional upon whether a given macro name is defined.

Syntax:

```
#ifdef name
#ifndef name
```

The #ifdef directive is "true" if *name* is defined, and the #ifndef directive is "true" if *name* is *not* defined. Both require a closing #endif directive.

The following two constructions are equivalent:

```
#ifdef VERSION
  ...
#endif

#if defined(VERSION)
  ...
#endif
```

#line

The compiler identifies errors it encounters during compilation by the source filename and the line number in the file. The #line directive can be used to change the filename and line numbering in the source file itself.

Syntax: #line new_number ["filename"]

From this location in the file onward, lines are counted starting from *new_number*. If *filename* is also specified, it becomes the new filename indicated by the compiler in any error messages.

The new filename must be enclosed in quotation marks, and *new_number* must be an integer constant.

Example:

```
#line 500 "my_prg.c"
```

The #line directive is typically used by program generators in translating other kinds of code into a C program. In this way the C compiler's error messages can be made to refer to the appropriate line and filename in the original source code.

The current effective line number and filename are accessible through the predefined macros __LINE__ and __FILE__.

Examples:

```
printf( "Current source line number: %d\n", __LINE__ );
printf ( "Source file: %s\n", __FILE__ );
```

#pragma

The #pragma directive is *implementation-specific*. It can be used to define any preprocessor directives desired for a given compiler.

Syntax: #pragma *command*

Any compiler that does not recognize *command* simply ignores the #pragma directive.

Example:

```
#pragma pack(1)
```

The Microsoft C compiler interprets this directive as an instruction to align the members of structures on byte boundaries, so that no unnamed gaps occur. (Other pragmas supported by that compiler are pack(2) and pack(4), for word and double-word alignment.)

ANSI C99 introduces the standard pragmas CX_LIMITED_RANGE, FENV_ACCESS, and FP_CONTRACT, which are described in the upcoming section "Mathematical Functions."

Predefined standard macros

There are eight predefined macros in C, whose names begin and end with two underline characters. They are described in Table 21.

Table 21. Predefined standard macros

Macro	Replacement value
__LINE__	The number of the line (within the given source file) in which the macro __LINE__ appears
__FILE__	The name of the source file in which the macro __FILE__ appears
__func__ (*)	The name of the function in which the macro __func__ appears
__DATE__	The date of compilation, in the format "Mmm dd yyyy". Example: "Dec 18 2002"
__TIME__	The time of compilation, in the format "hh:mm:ss"
__STDC__	The integer constant 1 if the compiler conforms to the ANSI standard

Table 21. Predefined standard macros (continued)

Macro	Replacement value
`__STD_HOSTED__` (*)	The integer constant 1 if the current implementation is a "hosted" implementation; otherwise 0
`__STD_VERSION__` (*)	The integer constant 199901L if the implementation conforms to C99, the ANSI C standard of January, 1999

ANSI C99 distinguishes between "hosted" and "free-standing" execution environments for C programs. Unlike the normal "hosted" environment, a "freestanding" environment provides only the capabilities of the standard library as declared in the header files *float.h*, *iso646.h*, *limits.h*, *stdarg.h*, *stdbool.h*, and *stddef.h*.

Standard Library

The remaining sections in this book describe the contents of the ANSI C library. The standard functions, types, and macros are grouped according to their purpose and areas of application. This arrangement makes it easy to find less well-known functions and macros. Each section also supplies the background information needed in order to make efficient use of the library's capabilities. New data types, functions, and macros introduced in ANSI C99 are indicated by an asterisk in parentheses (*).

Standard Header Files

All function prototypes, macros, and types in the ANSI library are contained in one or more of the following standard header files:

assert.h	*inttypes.h*(*)	*signal.h*	*stdlib.h*
complex.h(*)	*iso646.h*(*)	*stdarg.h*	*string.h*
ctype.h	*limits.h*	*stdbool.h*(*)	*tgmath.h*(*)
errno.h	*locale.h*	*stddef.h*	*time.h*
fenv.h(*)	*math.h*	*stdint.h*(*)	*wchar.h*(*)
float.h	*setjmp.h*	*stdio.h*	*wctype.h*(*)

Because a standard "function" may also be implemented as a macro, your source files should contain no other declaration of a function once the appropriate header file has been included.

Table 22 describes some commonly used types. The table also lists which header files define each type.

Table 22. Commonly used types

Type	Purpose	Header files
size_t	Used to express the size of an object as a number of bytes (generally equivalent to unsigned int)	stddef.h, stdio.h
wchar_t	Used to hold multi-byte character codes, and large enough to represent the codes of all extended character sets	stdlib.h, wchar.h[*]
wint_t[*]	An integer type used to represent wide characters, including the macro WEOF	wchar.h[*]
ptrdiff_t	Used to represent the difference of two pointers (usually equivalent to int)	stddef.h

Input and Output

The ANSI library provides a suite of high-level functions to manage all kinds of input and output, with the appropriate buffering, as uniform data streams.

When a file is opened, for example, a new stream is created along with a *file pointer*, which is a pointer to a structure of type FILE that contains information about the stream. This information includes the address of the buffer, the number of bytes not yet read, and other information about the file itself. The file pointer is used to identify the file in all subsequent operations.

Devices such as the display are addressed in the same way as files. When the program starts, three streams are open by default, with the following file pointers:

stdin
    The standard input device

stdout
    The standard output device

stderr
    The standard output device for error messages

stdin is generally associated with the keyboard, while stdout and stderr are associated with the display, unless redirection has been performed using the function freopen() or by the environment in which the program is running.

There is no predefined file structure in C: every file is assumed to contain simply a sequence of bytes. The internal structure of a file is completely left up to the program that uses it.

All read and write operations are applied at the current *file position*, which is the position of the next character to be read or written, and is always recorded in the FILE structure. When the file is opened, the file position is 0. It is increased by 1 with every character that is read or written. Random file access is achieved by means of functions that adjust the current file position.

In ANSI C99, characters in the extended character set can also be written to files. Thus any file used in read or write functions can be either *byte-oriented* or *wide-oriented*. After a file is opened and before any read or write access takes place, the file has no orientation. As soon as a byte input/output function is performed on the file, it becomes byte-oriented. If the first function that reads from or writes to the file is a wide-character input or output function, the file becomes wide-oriented. The function fwide() can also be used before the first access function to set the file's orientation, or to obtain its orientation at any time.

Only wide characters can be written to a wide-oriented file. The appropriate read and write functions thus perform conversion between wide characters with type wchar_t and the multibyte character encoding of the stream. For every wide-oriented stream, the momentary multibyte character parsing state is stored in an object with type mbstate_t. Byte access to wide-oriented files, and wide-character access to byte-oriented files, are not permitted.

Error Handling for Input/Output Functions

Errors on file access are indicated by the return value of the file access function. When the end of a file is encountered by a read function, for example, the symbolic constant EOF (for byte-oriented files) or WEOF (for wide-oriented files) is returned. If a read or write error has occurred, an error flag is also set in the FILE structure.

Furthermore, in reading or writing wide-oriented streams, errors can occur in the conversion between wide characters of type wchar_t and multibyte characters in the stream. This is the case if one of the conversion functions mbrtowc() and wcrtomb() does not return a permissible value. The global error variable errno then has the value EILSEQ ("error: illegal sequence").

General File Access Functions

The following functions, macros, and symbolic constants are declared in the header file *stdio.h*. In the descriptions below, *fp* designates the file pointer. Functions with type int return 0 to indicate success, or a value other than 0 in case of errors.

void **clearerr**(FILE *fp*);
    Clears the error and end-of-file flags.

int **fclose**(FILE *fp*);
    Closes the file.

int **feof**(FILE *fp*);
    Tests whether the end of the file has been reached. Returns a value not equal to 0 if the end-of-file flag is set, or 0 if it is not.

int **ferror**(FILE *fp);
    Tests whether an error occurred during file access.
    Returns a value not equal to 0 if the error flag is set, or 0
    if it is not.

int **fflush**(FILE *fp);
    Causes any unwritten data in the file buffer to be written
    to the file. Returns EOF if an error occurs, or 0 on success.

int **fgetpos**(FILE *fp, fpos_t *ppos);
    Determines the current file position and copies it to the
    variable addressed by *ppos*. The type fpos_t is generally
    defined as long.

FILE ***fopen**(const char *name, const char *mode);
    Opens the file *name* with the access mode *mode*. Possible
    access mode strings are "r" (read), "r+" (read and write),
    "w" (write), "w+" (write and read), "a" (append), and "a+"
    (append and read). For modes "r" and "r+", the file must
    already exist. Modes "w" and "w+" create a new file, or
    erase the contents of an existing file. Text or binary access
    mode can be specified by appending t or b to the mode
    string. If neither is used, the file is opened in text mode.

    The maximum length of a filename is the constant
    FILENAME_MAX. The maximum number of files that can be
    open simultaneously is FOPEN_MAX.

int **fsetpos**(FILE *fp, const fpos_t *ppos);
    Sets the file position to the new value referenced by *ppos*.

long **ftell**(FILE *fp);
    Returns the current file position.

FILE ***freopen**(const char *name, const char *mode,
                FILE *fp);
    Closes and reopens the file *name* with the access mode
    mode using the existing file pointer *fp*.

int **fseek**(FILE *fp, long offset, int origin);
    Moves the file position to *offset* bytes from the begin-
    ning of the file (if *origin* = SEEK_SET), or from the current

file position (if *origin* = SEEK_CUR), or from the end of the file (if *origin* = SEEK_END). The constants SEEK_SET, SEEK_CUR, and SEEK_END are usually defined as 0, 1, and 2.

void **perror**(const char *string*);
> After a system function call has resulted in an error, you can use perror() to write the string pointed to by *string* to stderr, followed by a colon and the appropriate system error message.

int **remove**(const char *filename*);
> Makes the file named *filename* unavailable by that name. If no other filenames are linked to the file, it is deleted.

int **rename**(const char *oldname*, const char *newname*);
> Changes the name of the file whose name is addressed by *oldname* to the string addressed by *newname*.

void **rewind**(FILE *fp*);
> Sets the file position to the beginning of the file, and clears the end-of-file and error flags.

void **setbuf**(FILE *fp*, char *buf*);
> Defines the array addressed by *buf* as the input/output buffer for the file. The buffer must be an array whose size is equal to the constant BUFSIZ. If *buf* is a null pointer, then the input/output stream is not buffered.

int **setvbuf**(FILE *fp*, char *buf*, int *mode*, size_t *sz*);
> Defines the array *buf* with length *sz* as the input/output buffer for the file. The parameter *mode* is one of the following constants: _IOFBF (full input/output buffering), _IOLBF (line-wise input/output buffering), or _IONBF (no input/output buffering). If *buf* is a null pointer, then a buffer of size *sz* is dynamically allocated.

FILE *tmpfile(void);
> Opens a temporary file in binary read/write mode. The file is automatically deleted at the end of the program. The program should be able to open at least TMP_MAX

temporary files. The symbolic constant TMP_MAX is greater than or equal to 25.

```
char *tmpnam( char *s );
```
Generates a unique filename that can be used to create a temporary file. If s is a null pointer, the filename generated is stored in an internal static buffer. Otherwise, s must point to a char array with a length of at least L_tmpnam bytes, in which the function stores the new name.

File Input/Output Functions

The classic functions for reading from and writing to files are declared in the header file *stdio.h*. In the descriptions that follow in Table 23, *fp* designates the file pointer. Those functions that have no parameter with the file pointer type read from stdin or write to stdout.

Reading and writing characters and strings

Table 23. Character read and write functions

Purpose	Functions
Write a character	int **fputc**(int c, FILE *fp); int **putc**(int c, FILE *fp); int **putchar**(int c);
Read a character	int **fgetc**(FILE *fp); int **getc**(FILE *fp); int **getchar**(void);
Put back a character	int **ungetc**(int c, FILE *fp);
Write a line	int **fputs**(const char *s, FILE *fp); int **puts**(const char *s);
Read a line	char ***fgets**(char *s, int n, FILE *fp); char ***gets**(char *buffer);

For each of these input/output functions, there is also a corresponding function for wide-oriented access. The wide functions are declared in the header file *wchar.h*(*). Their names are formed with wc (for *wide character*) in place of c (for *character*), or with ws (for *wide string*) in place of s (for *string*).

Block read and write functions

The following file access functions can be used to read or write a *block* of characters:

```
size_t fwrite( const void *buf, size_t sz, size_t n,
               FILE *fp );
```
Writes *n* objects of length *sz* from the buffer addressed by *buf* to the file.

```
size_t fread( void *buffer, size_t sz, size_t n,
              FILE *fp );
```
Reads up to *n* objects of length *sz* from the file and copies them to the memory location pointed to by *buf*.

Both functions return the number of objects transferred. If the return value is less than the argument *n*, then an error occurred, or fread() encountered the end of the file.

Formatted output

The printf functions provide *formatted* output:

```
int printf( const char *format, ... /*arg1, ... , argn*/ );
```
Writes the format string pointed to by *format* to the standard output stream, replacing conversion specifications with values from the argument list *arg1, ... , argn*.

```
int fprintf( FILE *fp, const char *format, ... );
```
Like printf(), but writes the format string *format* to the file indicated by the file pointer *fp*.

```
int vprintf( const char *format, va_list arg );
```
Like printf(), but with the variable argument list replaced by an object of type va_list that has been initialized using the va_start macro.

```
int vfprintf( FILE *fp, const char *format, va_list arg );
```
Like fprintf(), but with the variable argument list replaced by an object of type va_list that has been initialized using the va_start macro.

All of the `printf` functions return the number of characters written, or EOF if an error occurred.

In the following example, the function `printf()` is called with one conversion specification:

```
printf( "%+10.2f", sin( 1.2 ) );
```

The resulting output displays the signed value of $\sin(1.2)$ to two decimal places, right-justified in a field 10 spaces wide.

The general format of the *conversion specifications* used in the `printf` functions is as follows:

```
%[flags][field width][.precision]specifier
```

The *flags* consist of one or more of the characters +, ' ' (space), - , 0 , or #. Their meanings are:

+   The plus sign is prefixed to positive numbers.

' ' (space)
   A leading space is prefixed to positive numbers.

-    The output is left-justified in the field.

0   The field is filled with leading zeroes to the left of the number.

Alternate conversion rules are used as follows: If *specifier* is A(*), a(*), E, e, G, or g, floating-point numbers are formatted with a decimal point. If *specifier* is X, x, or o, hexadecimal integers are formatted with the 0X or 0x prefix, and octal integers with the 0 prefix.

The *field width* is a positive integer that fixes the length of the field occupied by the given conversion specification in the output string. If the *flags* include a minus sign, the converted value appears left-justified in the field; otherwise, it is right-justified. The excess field length is filled with space characters. If the output string is longer than the field width, the field width is increased as necessary to print the string in its entirety.

An asterisk (*) may also be specified for the field width. In this case, the field width is determined by an additional argument of type int, which immediately precedes the argument to be converted in the argument list.

.precision determines the number of decimal places printed in the output of *floating-point numbers,* when *specifier* is f or e. If *specifier* is g, *.precision* determines the number of significant digits. Rounding is performed if necessary. For floating-point numbers, the default value for *.precision* is 6.

For *integers,* *.precision* indicates the minimum number of digits to be printed. Leading zeroes are prefixed as necessary. For integers, the default value for *.precision* is 1.

If the argument to be converted is a *string,* then *.precision* indicates the maximum number of characters of the string that should appear.

specifier is the conversion specifier, indicating how the given argument is to be interpreted and converted. Note that *specifier* must correspond to the actual type of the argument to be converted. The possible conversion specifiers are listed in Table 24.

Table 24. Conversion specifiers for formatted output

Specifier	Argument types	Output format
d, i	int	Decimal
u	unsigned int	Decimal
o	unsigned int	Octal
x	unsigned int	Hexadecimal with a, b, c, d, e, f
X	unsigned int	Hexadecimal with A, B, C, D, E, F
f	float/double	Floating-point number, decimal
e, E	float/double	Exponential notation, decimal
a, A	float/double	Exponential notation, hexadecimal(*)
g, G	float/double	Floating-point or exponential notation, whichever is shorter
c	char / int	Single character

Table 24. Conversion specifiers for formatted output (continued)

Specifier	Argument types	Output format
s	string	The string terminated by '\0' or truncated to the number of characters specified by .*precision*.
N	int *	The number of characters printed up to this point is stored in the given location
p	pointer	The corresponding address, hexadecimal
%	none	The character %

The letter l (that's an ell) can be prefixed to the c or s conversion specifiers to indicate a *wide character* or a *wide string*.

The letters l or ll(*) can also be prefixed to the conversion specifiers d , i , u , o , x , and X to indicate an argument of type long or long long(*). Similarly, h or hh can be prefixed to the same conversion specifiers to indicate an argument of type short or char.

An argument of type long double can be converted by using the prefix L with the conversion specifier f , e , E , g , G , a, or A.

Furthermore, ANSI C99 has introduced the following extensions:

- The new conversion specifiers A and a can be used to print a number of type double in hexadecimal exponential notation (0Xh.hhhhP±d or 0xh.hhhhp±d). This conversion uses FLOAT_RADIX, which is generally defined as 2, as the base. If no precision is specified, the number is printed with as many hexadecimal numerals as necessary for exact representation.

- Arguments of type intmax_t(*) or uintmax_t(*) can be converted by prefixing the letter j to the conversion specifiers d, i, o, u, x, or X. Similarly, the argument type size_t is indicated by the prefix z, and the type ptrdiff_t by the prefix t.

- For the integer types defined in the header file *stdint.h*[*] (such as `int16_t` and `int_least32_t`), there are separate conversion specifiers for use in `printf()` format strings. These conversion specifiers are defined as macros in the header file `inttypes.h`[*]. The macro names for the conversion specifiers corresponding to d, i, o, x, and X begin with the prefixes PRId, PRIi, PRIo, PRIu, PRIx, and PRIX. For example, the macro names beginning with PRId are:

  PRId*N* PRIdLEAST*N* PRIdFAST*N* PRIdMAX PRIdPTR

  where *N* is the width in bits (usually 8, 16, 32, or 64). For example:

  ```
  intmax_t i = INTMAX_MAX;
  printf("Largest integer value: %20" PRIdMAX "\n",i );
  ```

Formatted input

The `scanf()` input functions are the counterparts to the `printf()` formatted output functions. They are used to read file input under control of a format string and convert the information for assignment to variables.

int **scanf**(const char *format*, ... /**arg1*, ... , *argn*/);
  Reads characters from standard input and saves the converted values in the variables *addressed* by the pointer arguments *arg1*, ... , *argn*. The characters read are converted according to the conversion specifications in the format string *format*.

int **fscanf**(FILE *fp*, const char *format*, ...);
  Like scanf(), but reads from the file specified by *fp* rather than standard input.

int **vfscanf**(FILE *fp*, const char *format*, va_list *arg*);
  Like fscanf(), but with the variable argument list replaced by an object (*arg*) of type va_list that has been initialized using the va_start macro. See "Functions with Variable Numbers of Arguments" earlier in this book for information on va_list and va_start.

```
int vscanf( const char *format, va_list arg );
```
Like scanf(), but with the variable argument list replaced by an object (*arg*) of type va_list that has been initialized using the va_start macro. See "Functions with Variable Numbers of Arguments" earlier in this book for information on va_list and va_start.

All of the scanf functions return the number of successfully converted input fields. The return value is EOF if the first input field could not be read or converted, or if the end of the input file was reached.

The general format of the *conversion specifications* used in the scanf functions is as follows:

```
%[field width]specifier
```

For example:

```
scanf( "%5d", &var );   // var has type int
```

For each conversion specification in the format string, the next *input item* is read, converted, and assigned to the variable *pointed to by* the corresponding argument. Input fields are separated by whitespace characters (space, tab, and newline characters).

field width indicates the maximum number of characters to be read and converted. The next input field begins with the first character not yet processed.

specifier corresponds to the conversion specifiers in output format strings, except for the following differences:

- %i is used to read decimal, octal, and hexadecimal integers. The base is determined by the number's prefix, as for constants in source code.

- %f converts input for assignment to a variable of type float, and %lf to a variable of type double.

- %c reads the next character, which may also be a space. All other conversion specifiers read the next input item, skipping over any spaces that precede it.

- %s reads a string and appends the string terminator character '\0'. The conversion specifier for a string, s, may be replaced by a sequence of characters in square brackets, called the *scanlist*. In this case, each character read must match one of these characters. For example, use %[1234567890] to read only digits. The first character that does not match any of the characters in the scanlist terminates the input item. If the scanlist begins with a caret (^), then the input item is terminated by the first character in the input stream that *does* match one of the other characters in the scanlist. A hyphen can be used to indicate a sequence of consecutive search characters. For example, the scanlist [a-f] is equivalent to [abcdef].

If a conversion specification contains an asterisk (*) after the percent sign (%), then the input item is read as specified, but not assigned to a variable. In effect, that input field is skipped. Such a conversion specification corresponds to *no* variable argument.

Any character that cannot be interpreted according to the conversion specification terminates the current input field, and is put back into the input buffer. This character is then the first one read for the next input item.

The format string can also contain other characters that do not form part of a conversion specification and are *not* *whitespace*. The scanf functions expect such characters to be matched in the input stream, but do not convert or save them. If non-matching characters occur in the input, the function stops reading from the file. However, a whitespace character in the format string matches any sequence of whitespace characters in the input. For example, if the format string " %c" is used to read an individual character, any leading whitespace is skipped.

As for printf(), ANSI C99 defines separate conversion specifiers for reading fixed-width integer variables, such as int_least32_t. The corresponding macro names, defined in the header file *inttypes.h*(*), have the prefix SCN (for "scan") rather than PRI (for "print").

The header file *wchar.h*(*) contains the declarations of wprintf(), wscanf(), and related functions. These functions provide input and output controlled by a wide format string. The conversion specifications and their interpretation are identical to those of the printf() and scanf() functions.

Numerical Limits and Number Classification

When working with C's various numeric types, it's important to understand the range of values that each type can hold.

Value Ranges of Integer Types

The value ranges of the *integer* types are documented in the header file *limits.h*. The constants, listed in Table 25, indicate the largest and smallest values that can be represented by the given type.

Table 25. Limits of the integer types

Type	Minimum	Maximum	Maximum of the unsigned type
char	CHAR_MIN	CHAR_MAX	UCHAR_MAX
signed char	SCHAR_MIN	SCHAR_MAX	
short	SHRT_MIN	SHRT_MAX	USHRT_MAX
int	INT_MIN	INT_MAX	UINT_MAX
long	LONG_MIN	LONG_MAX	ULONG_MAX
long long(*)	LLONG_MIN(*)	LLONG_MAX(*)	ULLONG_MAX(*)

If char is interpreted as signed, then CHAR_MIN is equal to SCHAR_MIN and CHAR_MAX is equal to SCHAR_MAX. If not, then CHAR_MIN is equal to 0 and CHAR_MAX is equal to UCHAR_MAX.

In addition to the constants listed in Table 25, *limits.h* also contains the following:

CHAR_BIT
    The number of bits in a byte (usually 8)

MB_LEN_MAX
    The maximum number of bytes in a multibyte character

In the header file *stdint.h*(*), constants are also defined to document the minimum and maximum values of the types wchar_t, wint_t, size_t, ptrdiff_t, and sig_atomic_t, and of the fixed-width integer types, such as int_least32_t. The names of these constants are formed from the type names as follows: the type name is written all in capital letters, and the suffix _t is replaced by _MIN or _MAX. For example:

```
WCHAR_MIN         // Minimum value of wchar_t
INT_LEAST32_MAX   // Maximum value of int_least32_t
```

For the unsigned types only the ..._MAX constants are defined.

Range and Precision of Real Floating Types

The macros listed in Table 26 are defined in the header file *float.h* to represent the range and the precision of the types float, double, and long double. The macro names are formed using the prefixes FLT for float, DBL for double, and LDBL for long double. The macros FLT_RADIX and FLT_ROUNDS apply to all three floating types.

Table 26. Macros for floating types in float.h

Macro name	Purpose
FLT_RADIX	Base (or radix) of the exponential notation
FLT_ROUNDS	Indicates how rounding is performed on values that cannot be represented exactly: −1 = undetermined 0 = towards zero, 1 = towards the nearest representable value 2 = upwards 3 = downwards

Table 26. Macros for floating types in float.h (continued)

Macro name	Purpose
FLT_MANT_DIG DBL_MANT_DIG LDBL_MANT_DIG	The number of digits in the mantissa to base FLT_RADIX
FLT_MIN_EXP DBL_MIN_EXP LDBL_MIN_EXP	Minimum value of the exponent to base FLT_RADIX
FLT_MAX_EXP DBL_MAX_EXP LDBL_MAX_EXP	Maximum value of the exponent to base FLT_RADIX

The macros listed in Table 26 document the range and precision of all real floating types. In actual programs, such information is most often needed for *decimal* (base 10) notation. Accordingly, you can use the macros for type float listed Table 27, and which are defined in *float.h*.

Table 27. Limits for the type float

Macro name	Purpose
FLT_DIG	Precision as a number of decimal digits
FLT_MIN_10_EXP	Minimum negative exponent to base 10
FLT_MAX_10_EXP	Maximum positive exponent to base 10
FLT_MIN	Minimum representable positive floating-point number
FLT_MAX	Maximum representable floating-point number
FLT_EPSILON	Minimum positive representable floating-point number x such that $1.0 + x \mathrel{!=} 1.0$

Similar constants are also defined for the types double and long double. These have names beginning with DBL or LDBL in place of FLT.

ANSI C99 also introduces the macro DECIMAL_DIG, which indicates the precision of the largest floating type as a number of decimal digits.

Classification of Floating-Point Numbers

ANSI C99 defines five categories of floating-point numbers, listed in Table 28. A symbolic constant for each category is defined in the header file *math.h*.

Table 28. Floating-point categories

Macro name	Category
FP_ZERO	Floating-point numbers with the value 0
FP_NORMAL	Floating-point numbers in normalized representation
FP_SUBNORMAL[a]	Floating-point numbers in subnormal representation
FP_INFINITE	Floating-point numbers that represent an infinite value
FP_NAN	Not a Number (NAN): bit patterns that do not represent a valid floating-point number

[a] Tiny numbers may be represented in subnormal notation.

The macros in Table 29 can be used to classify a real floating-point number x with respect to the categories in Table 28 without causing an error condition.

Table 29. Macros for floating-point number classification

Macro	Result
fpclassify(x)	Returns one of the constants described in Table 28 to indicate the category to which x belongs.
isfinite(x)	Returns "true" (i.e., a value other than 0) if the value of x is finite (0, normal, subnormal, not infinite, or NAN), otherwise 0.
isinf(x)	Returns "true" if x is an infinity, otherwise 0.
isnormal(x)	Returns "true" if the value of x is a normalized floating-point number not equal to 0. Returns 0 in all other cases.
isnan(x)	Returns "true" if x is "not a number" (NaN), otherwise 0.
signbit(x)	Returns "true" if x is negative (i.e., if the sign bit is set), otherwise 0

The following constants are also defined in *math.h*:

INFINITY
   The maximum positive value of type float, used to represent infinity.

NAN *(Not a Number)*
   A value of type `float` which is not a valid floating-point number.

NANs can be either *quiet* or *signaling*. If a signaling NAN occurs in the evaluation of an arithmetic expression, the exception status flag `FE_INVALID` in the floating point environment is set. This flag is not set when a quiet NAN occurs.

C implementations are not required to support the concept of NANs. If NANs are not supported, the constant NAN is not defined.

Mathematical Functions

C supports a variety of useful mathematical functions. Different functions apply to different datatypes. For example, randomization functions apply to integers, whereas trigonometric functions apply to floating-point values.

Mathematical Functions for Integer Types

The mathematical functions for the types `int` and `long` are declared in *stdlib.h*.

`int **rand**( void );`
   Generates a random number between 0 and `RAND_MAX`. The constant `RAND_MAX` has a value of at least 32767, or $2^{15} - 1$.

`void **srand**( unsigned n );`
   Initializes the random number generator with the seed *n*. After this function has been called, calls to `rand()` generate a new sequence of random numbers.

`int **abs**( int x );`
   Returns the absolute value of *x*.

`div_t **div**( int x, int y );`
   Divides *x* by *y* and stores the integer part of the quotient and the remainder in a structure of type `div_t`, whose

members quot (the quotient) and rem (the remainder) have type int. The type div_t is defined in *stdlib.h*.

The corresponding (to abs() and div()) functions labs(), llabs()[(*)], lldiv()[(*)], and ldiv() are also provided for integers of type long or long long(*). Furthermore, the functions imaxabs()[(*)] and imaxdiv()[(*)] are defined for the type intmax_t[(*)]. These functions are declared in *inttypes.h*[(*)].

Mathematical Functions for Real Floating Types

The mathematical functions declared in *math.h* were originally defined only for double values, with return values and parameters of type double. These functions are shown in Table 30.

Table 30. The traditional mathematical functions for double values

Mathematical function	C function
Trigonometric functions:	
Sine, cosine, tangent	sin(), cos(), tan()
Arcsine, arccosine	asin(), acos()
Arctangent	atan(), atan2()
Hyperbolic functions	sinh(), cosh(), tanh()
Powers, square root	pow(), sqrt(),
Exponential functions	exp(), frexp(), ldexp()
Logarithms	log(), log10()
Next integer	ceil(), floor()
Absolute value	fabs()
Remainder (modular division)	fmod()
Separation of integer and fractional parts	modf()

ANSI C99 introduces new versions of the functions listed in Table 30 for the types `float` and `long double`. The names of these functions end with f or l; for example:

```
double cos( double x );
float cosf( float x );
long double cosl( long double x );
```

New standard mathematical functions for real numbers have also been added in *math.h*, as listed in Table 31. These functions also have versions for `float` and `long double`, with names ending in f and l.

Table 31. New mathematical functions for double values in ANSI C99

Mathematical function	C function
Trigonometric functions	`asinh()`, `acosh()`, `atanh()`
Exponential functions	`exp2()`, `expm1()`
Logarithms	`ilogb()`, `logb()`, `log1p()`, `log2()`
Roots	`cbrt()`, `hypot()`
Remainder	`remainder()`, `remquo()`
Positive difference	`fdim()`
Minimum and maximum	`fmin()`, `fmax()`
Rounding	`trunc()`, `rint()`, `lrint()`, `llrint()`, `round()`, `lround()`, `llround()`
Next number	`nearbyint()`, `nextafter()`, `nexttoward()`
Copy sign	`copysign()`
Optimized operations	`scalbn()`, `scalbln()`, `fma()`
Gamma function	`tgamma()`, `lgamma()`
Error functions	`erf()`, `erfc()`

Macros for comparing floating-point numbers are also defined in *math.h* and are listed in Table 32. Unlike the comparative operators, these macros do not raise the `FE_INVALID` exception when the arguments cannot be compared, as when one of them is a `NAN`, for example.

Table 32. Macros for comparing floating-point numbers

Macro	Comparative expression
isgreater(x, y)	$(x) > (y)$
isgreaterequal(x, y)	$(x) >= (y)$
isless(x, y)	$(x) < (y)$
islessequal(x, y)	$(x) <= (y)$
islessgreater(x, y)	$(x) < (y)$ || $(x) > (y)$
isunordered(x, y)	1 if x and y cannot be compared, otherwise 0

Optimizing Runtime Efficiency

ANSI C99 has introduced features to optimize the efficiency of floating-point operations.

The types float_t and double_t, defined in *math.h*, represent the types used internally in floating-point arithmetic. When these types are used in a program, no conversions are necessary before arithmetic operations are performed. The macro FLT_EVAL_METHOD indicates what the equivalent basic types are, and returns one of the values described in Table 33.

Table 33. Interpretation of float_t and double_t

FLT_EVAL_METHOD	Type represented by float_t	Type represented by double_t
0	float	double
1	double	double
2	long double	long double

CPUs may have special machine instructions to perform standard arithmetic operations quickly. Rounding and error conditions may also be ignored. Optimizations of these kinds can be enabled by the pragma FP_CONTRACT. For example:

```
#pragma  STDC FP_CONTRACT ON
```

The same pragma with the switch OFF rather than ON disables such optimizations.

Furthermore, the macro FP_FAST_FMA is defined if the "float-ing-point multiply-add" function fma(x, y, z), which returns x*y+z, is implemented as a special instruction, and is thus faster than separate multiplication and addition opera-tions. The macros FP_FAST_FMAF and FP_FAST_FMAL are analo-gous indicators for the functions fmaf() and fmal().

Mathematical Functions for Complex Floating Types

Functions and macros for complex numbers are declared in the header file *complex.h*(*). The functions shown in Table 34 have one parameter and return a value of type double complex.

Table 34. Mathematical functions for the type double complex

Mathematical function	C function
Trigonometric functions:	
Sine, cosine, tangent	csin(), ccos(), ctan()
Arcsine, arccosine	casin(), cacos()
Arctangent	catan()
Hyperbolic functions	csinh(), ccosh(), ctanh(), casinh(), cacosh(), catanh()
Powers, square root	cpow(), csqrt()
Exponential function	cexp()
Logarithm	clog()
Complex conjugate	conj()

The functions shown in Table 35 have one parameter of type double complex and return a value of type double.

Table 35. Complex functions with type double

Mathematical function	C function
Absolute value	cabs()
Argument (phase angle)	carg()

Table 35. Complex functions with type double (continued)

Mathematical function	C function
Real and imaginary parts	`creal()`, `cimag()`
Projection onto the Riemann sphere	`cproj()`

These functions also have versions for `float complex` and `long double complex`, with names ending in f and l.

Table 36 shows macros that are defined for complex types.

Table 36. Macros for complex types

Macro	Replacement value
`complex`	`_Complex`
`_Complex_I`	The imaginary unit, i.e., the number i such that $i^2 = -1$, with type `const float _Complex`
`imaginary`	`_Imaginary`
`_Imaginary_I`	The imaginary unit, with type `const float _Imaginary`
`I`	`_Imaginary_I` if the compiler supports the type `_Imaginary`, otherwise `_Complex_I`

Arithmetic operations with complex numbers can be accelerated in cases when no overflow or underflow can occur. The programmer can signal such "safe" operations using the pragma:

```
#pragma STDC CX_LIMITED_RANGE ON
```

The default setting is OFF.

Type-Generic Macros

The *type-generic macros* defined in header file *tgmath.h* are unified names that can be used to call the different mathematical functions for specific real and complex floating types.

If a given function is defined for real or for both real and complex floating types, then the type-generic macro name is the same as the name of the function version with type double. (The real function `modf()` is an exception, however, for which there is no type-generic macro.)

The type-generic macros always call the function that matches the type of the arguments. For example:

```
complex z = 1.0 + 2.1*I;
cos( z );      // Calls ccos()
ceil( 7.1L );  // Calls ceill()
```

Type-generic macros are also defined for the complex functions for which there are no corresponding real functions: `carg()`, `conj()`, `creal()`, `cimag()`, and `cproj()`. These macros always call the corresponding complex function, if the argument is a real floating-point number or a complex number.

Error Handling for Mathematical Functions

Error conditions are customarily detected by examining the return value of a function and/or the global error variable `errno`. The variable `errno` is declared with type `int` in the header file *errno.h*.

If a function is passed an argument that is outside the domain for which the function is defined, a "domain error" occurs, and `errno` is assigned the value of the macro `EDOM`. Similarly, if the result of a function cannot be represented by the type of the function's return value, then a "range error" occurs, and `errno` is assigned the value `ERANGE`. In the case of an overflow—that is, if the magnitude of the result is too great for the specified type—the function returns the value of the macro `HUGE_VAL`, with the appropriate sign. In case of an underflow—i.e., the magnitude of the result is too small—the function returns 0.

In addition to `HUGE_VAL` (with type `double`), ANSI C99 also provides the macros `HUGE_VALF` (type `float`) and `HUGE_VALL` (type `long double`), which are returned by functions of the corresponding types.

Furthermore, ANSI C99 introduces the macros FP_ILOGB0 and FP_ILOGBNAN. The function ilogb(x) returns FP_ILOGB0 if x is equal to 0. If x is "not a number" (NaN), ilogb(x) returns the value of FP_ILOGBNAN.

The Floating-Point Environment

ANSI C99 has introduced the *floating-point environment* to permit more detailed representation of error conditions in floating-point arithmetic. All of the declarations for the floating-point environment are contained in the header file *fenv.h*[*]. The floating-point environment contains two system variables: one for the status flags, which are used in handling *floating-point exceptions*, and one for the *control modes*, which determine certain behaviors of floating-point arithmetic, such as the rounding method used.

For every exception possible in an implementation that supports floating-point exceptions, an appropriate status flag is defined, as described in Table 37.

Table 37. Macros for floating-point exceptions in fenv.h[*]

Macro	Error condition
FE_DIVBYZERO	Division by 0
FE_INEXACT	The result of the operation is not exact
FE_INVALID	The result is undefined, e.g., a value was outside the domain for which the function is defined
FE_OVERFLOW	A floating-point overflow occurred
FE_UNDERFLOW	An underflow occurred

Several of these constants can be combined by a bitwise OR (|). The macro FE_ALL_EXCEPT is equal to the bitwise OR of all of the floating-point exception constants implemented. The system variable for the floating-point exception status has the type fexcept_t.

The following functions are used to handle floating-point exceptions. With the exception of `fetestexcept()`, each function returns 0 to indicate success, or a value other than 0 in case of errors. The *excepts* argument indicates which of the exceptions listed in Table 37 are affected.

`int fetestexcept( int excepts );`
> Tests which of the specified floating-point exceptions are set. Bits are set in the return value to correspond to the exceptions that are currently set.

`int feclearexcept( int excepts );`
> Clears the specified floating-point exceptions.

`int feraiseexcept( int excepts );`
> Raises the specified floating-point exceptions.

`int fegetexceptflag( fexcept_t *flagp, int excepts );`
> Saves the status of the specified exceptions in the object referenced by *flagp*.

`int fesetexceptflag( const fexcept_t *flagp,`
`                     int excepts );`
> Sets the exception status according to the flags previously saved (by `fegetexceptflag()`) in the object referenced by *flagp*.

The *control mode* determines certain properties of floating-point arithmetic, including the rounding method used. The symbolic constants described in Table 38 are defined for this purpose.

Table 38. Controlling rounding behavior

Macro	Rounding direction
FE_DOWNWARD	Round down to the next lower value.
FE_TONEAREST	Round to the nearest value.
FE_TOWARDZERO	Truncate.
FE_UPWARD	Round up to the next higher value.

The current rounding direction can be read and changed using the functions int fegetround() and int fesetround(int *round*).

The following functions manipulate the floating-point environment as a single entity. The type fenv_t represents the entire floating-point environment.

int **fegetenv**(fenv_t *envp*);
 Saves the current floating-point environment in the object referenced by *envp*.

int **fesetenv**(const fenv_t *envp*);
 Establishes the floating-point environment referenced by *envp*.

int **feholdexcept**(fenv_t *envp*);
 Saves the current floating-point environment in the object referenced by *envp*, then clears the status flags and installs a *non-stop mode*, so that processing continues in case of further floating-point exceptions.

int **feupdateenv**(const fenv_t *envp*);
 Establishes the floating-point environment referenced by *envp*, and then raises the exceptions that were set in the saved environment.

The macro FE_DFL_ENV is a pointer to the floating-point environment that is installed at program start-up, and can be used as an argument in the functions fesetenv() and feupdateenv().

The floating-point environment need not be active in an implementation that supports it. It can be activated by the pragma:

```
#pragma STDC FENV_ACCESS ON
```

and deactivated by the same pragma with the switch OFF.

The macro math_errhandling, defined in *math.h*, can be used to determine whether the program uses errno and/or the floating-point environment:

- If the expression math_errhandling & MATH_ERRNO is not 0, then the error variable errno is used.
- If the expression math_errhandling & MATH_ERREXCEPT is not 0, then floating-point errors raise the exceptions defined in *fenv.h*.

Character Classification and Case Mapping

A number of functions for classifying and changing the case of characters with type char are defined in the header file *ctype.h*. These functions, whose names begin with is... or to..., accept a one-character argument whose value is between 0 and 255, or EOF.

The is... functions, listed in Table 39, test whether the character is a member of a specific category of characters. They return "true," i.e., a non-zero value, if the character is in the given category. If not, the return value is 0, or "false."

Table 39. Functions for character classification

Category	Function
Letter	int **isalpha**(int c);
Lower-case letter	int **islower**(int c);
Upper-case letter	int **isupper**(int c);
Decimal digit	int **isdigit**(int c);
Hexadecimal digit	int **isxdigit**(int c);
Letter or decimal digit	int **isalnum**(int c);
Printable character	int **isprint**(int c);
Printable character other than space ' '	int **isgraph**(int c);
Whitespace character	int **isspace**(int c);

Table 39. Functions for character classification (continued)

Category	Function
Punctuation mark	`int ispunct( int c );`
Control character	`int iscntrl( int c );`
Space or horizontal tabulator	`int isblank( int c );`(*)

The following example reads a character and then tests to see whether it is a digit:

```
int c = getchar();    // Read a character
if ( isdigit( c ) ) ...// Is it a decimal digit?
```

The `to...` functions are used to convert characters from upper- to lower-case and vice versa, as shown in Table 40.

Table 40. Case mapping functions

Conversion	Function
Upper- to lower-case	`int tolower( int c );`
Lower- to upper-case	`int toupper( int c );`

The corresponding functions for wide characters, with type `wchar_t`, are declared in the header file *wctype.h*(*). Their names are similar to those in Tables 39 and 40, but start with `isw...` and `tow...`. These functions expect one character argument of type `wint_t` whose value is between 0 and 32767, or `WEOF`.

For wide characters there are also the *extensible* classification and mapping functions, `iswctype()` and `towctrans()`. These functions provide flexible, locale-specific testing and mapping of wide characters. Before one of these functions is used, the desired test criterion or mapping information must be registered by a call to `wctype()` or `wctrans()`:

```
iswctype( wc, wctype( "lower" ));
towctrans( wc, wctrans( "upper" ));
```

These calls are equivalent to iswlower(wc); and towupper(wc);. The function wctype() returns a value of type wctype_t, and wctrans() has a return value of type wctrans_t.

Single-byte characters of type unsigned char can be converted to the type wchar_t using the function btowc(), which is declared in *wchar.h*[*]. The opposite conversion is performed by the function wctob(). If the character cannot be converted, these functions return EOF or WEOF.

All of these functions take language-specific particularities of the current locale into account (see the later section "Internationalization").

String Handling

There is no basic type for strings in C. A string is simply a sequence of characters ending with the string terminator, stored in a char array. A string is represented by a char pointer that points to the first character in the string.

The customary functions for manipulating strings are declared in *string.h*. Those functions that modify a string return a pointer to the modified string. The functions used to search for a character or a substring return a pointer to the occurrence found, or a null pointer if the search was unsuccessful.

char *__strcat__(char *s1, const char *s2);
> Appends the string s2 to the end of s1. The first character copied from s2 replaces the string terminator character of s1.

char *__strchr__(const char *s, int c);
> Locates the first occurrence of the character c in the string s.

int __strcmp__(const char *s1, const char *s2);
> Compares the strings s1 and s2, and returns a value that is greater than, equal to, or less than 0 to indicate

whether s1 is greater than, equal to, or less than s2. A string is greater than another if the first character code in it which differs from the corresponding character code in the other string is greater than that character code.

int **strcoll**(const char *s1, const char *s2);
Transforms an internal copy of the strings s1 and s2 using the function strxfrm(), then compares them using strcmp() and returns the result.

char ***strcpy**(char *s1, const char *s2);
Copies s2 to the char array referenced by s1. This array must be large enough to contain s2 including its string terminator character '\0'.

int **strcspn**(const char *s1, const char *s2);
Determines the length of the maximum initial substring of s1 that contains none of the characters found in s2.

size_t **strlen**(const char *s);
Returns the length of the string addressed by s. The length of the string is the number of characters it contains, excluding the string terminator character '\0'.

char ***strncat**(char *s1, const char *s2, size_t n);
Appends the first n characters of s2 (and the string terminator character) to s1.

int **strncmp**(const char *s1, const char *s2, size_t n);
Compares the first n characters of the strings s1 and s2. The return value is the same as for strcmp().

char ***strncpy**(char *s1, const char *s2, size_t n);
Copies the first n characters of s2 to the char array s1. The string terminator character '\0' is not appended. If s2 is a string that is shorter than n characters, the remaining characters written are '\0'.

char ***strpbrk**(const char *s1, const char *s2);
Locates the first occurrence in s1 of any of the characters contained in s2.

```
char *strrchr( const char *s, int c );
```
Locates the last occurrence of the character c in the string s. The string terminator character '\0' is included in the search.

```
int strspn( const char *s1, const char *s2 );
```
Determines the length of the maximum initial substring of s1 that consists only of characters contained in s2.

```
char *strstr( const char *s1, const char *s2 );
```
Locates the first occurrence of s2 (without the terminating '\0') in s1.

```
char *strtok( char *s1, const char *s2 );
```
Breaks the string in s1 into the substrings ("tokens") delimited by any of the characters contained in s2.

```
size_t strxfrm( char *s1, const char *s2, size_t n );
```
Performs a locale-specific transformation (such as a case conversion) of s2 and copies the result to the char array with length n that is referenced by s1.

Similar functions for wide-character strings, declared in the header file wchar.h(*), have names beginning with wcs in place of str.

Conversion Between Strings and Numbers

A variety of functions are declared in the header file stdlib.h to obtain numerical interpretations of the initial digit characters in a string. The resulting number is the return value of the function.

```
int atoi( const char *s );
```
Interprets the contents of the string s as a number with type int. The analogous functions atol(), atoll()(*), and atof() are used to convert a string into a number with type long, long long(*), or double.

```
double strtod( const char *s, char **pptr );
```
Serves a similar purpose to that of atof(), but takes the address of a char pointer as a second argument. If the char pointer referenced by *pptr* is not NULL, it is set to the first character in the string *s* (excluding any leading whitespace) that is not part of the substring representing a floating-point number.

The corresponding functions for conversion to the types float and long double are strtof()[*] and strtold()[*].

```
long strtol( const char *s, char **pptr, int base );
```
Converts a string to a number with type long. The third parameter is the base of the numeral string, and may be an integer between 2 and 36, or 0. If *base* is 0, the string *s* is interpreted as a numeral in base 8, 16, or 10, depending on whether it begins with 0, 0x, or one of the digits 1 to 9.

The analogous functions for converting a string to unsigned long, long long[*] or unsigned long long[*] are strtoul()[*], strtoll()[*], and strtoull()[*].

The header file *inttypes.h*[*] also declares the functions strtoimax() and strtoumax(), which convert the initial digits in a string to an integer of type intmax_t or uintmax_t.

Similar functions for wide-character strings are declared in the header file *wchar.h*[*]. Their names begin with wcs in place of str.

The following function from the printf family is used to convert numeric values into a formatted numeral string:

```
int sprintf(char *s,const char *format,.../*a1,...,an*/);
```
Copies the format string *format* to the char array referenced by *s*, with the conversion specifications replaced using the values in the argument list *a1,...,an*.

Numerical values can also be read from a string based on a format string:

```
int sscanf(char *s,const char *format,.../*a1,...,an*/);
```
    Reads and converts data from s, and copies the resulting
    values to the locations addressed by the argument list
    a1,...,an.

The functions vsprintf() and vsscanf() are similar to
sprintf() and sscanf(), but with the variable argument list
replaced by an object of type va_list that has been initialized using the va_start macro (see "Functions with Variable
Numbers of Arguments" earlier in this book). The functions
snprintf() and vsnprintf() write a maximum of *n* characters, including the string terminator character, to the array
referenced by s. These functions return the number of characters actually written to the array, not counting the string
terminator character.

The corresponding formatted string input/output functions
for wide-character strings are declared in *wchar.h*(*). Their
names begin with sw (for "string, wide") in place of the initial s (for "string") in the names of the functions described
above for char strings. For example, swprintf().

Multibyte Character Conversion

A multibyte character may occupy more than one byte in
memory. The maximum number of bytes that can be used to
represent a multibyte character is the value of the macro MB_
CUR_MAX, which is defined in *stdlib.h*. Its value is dependent
on the current locale. In the default locale "C", MB_CUR_MAX
has the value 1.

Every multibyte character corresponds to exactly one character of type wchar_t. The functions for multibyte character
conversion are declared in the header file *stdlib.h*.

```
int mblen( const char *s, size_t max );
```
    Determines the length of the multibyte character pointed
    to by s. The maximum length of the character is specified
    by *max*. Accordingly, *max* must not exceed MB_CUR_MAX.

```
size_t wctomb( char *s, wchar_t wc );
```
> Converts the wide character *wc* into the multibyte repre-
> sentation, and writes the corresponding multibyte char-
> acter in the array addressed by *s*.

```
size_t wcstombs( char *s, const wchar_t *p, size_t n );
```
> Converts the first *n* wide characters referenced by *p* into
> multibyte characters, and copies the results to the char
> array addressed by *s*.

```
size_t mbtowc( wchar_t *p, const char *s, size_t max );
```
> Determines the wide character code corresponding to the
> multibyte character in *s*, whose maximum length is spec-
> ified by *max*, and copies the result to the wchar_t variable
> referenced by *p*.

```
size_t mbstowcs( wchar_t *p, const char *s, size_t n );
```
> Converts the first *n* multibyte characters of *s* into the
> wide characters and copies the result to the array
> addressed by *p*.

Similar functions with an additional r in their names (for
restartable) are also declared in *wchar.h*(*). The restartable
functions have an additional parameter, a pointer to the type
mbstate_t, that must point to an object describing the current wide/multibyte character conversion state. Furthermore, the function mbsinit()(*) can be used to test whether
the current conversion state is an initial conversion state.

Searching and Sorting

The following two functions are declared in the header file
stdlib.h as general utilities for searching and sorting:

```
void qsort(void *a, size_t n, size_t size,
           int (*compare)(const void *,const void *));
```
> Sorts the array *a* using the quick-sort algorithm. The
> array is assumed to have *n* elements whose size is *size*.

```
void *bsearch( const void *key, const void *a,
               size_t n, size_t size, int
               (*compare)( const void*, const void* ) );
```
Searches in a sorted array *a* for the key addressed by *key*, using the binary search algorithm. The array *a* is assumed to have *n* array elements whose size is *size*.

The last parameter to these functions, *compare*, is a pointer to a function that compares two elements of the array a. Usually this function must be defined by you, the programmer. Its parameters are two pointers to the array elements to be compared. The function must return a value that is less than, equal to, or greater than 0 to indicate whether the first element is less than, equal to, or greater than the second. To search or sort an array of float values, for example, the following comparison function could be specified:

```
int floatcmp( const void* p1, const void* p2 )
{  float x = *(float *)p1,
         y = *(float *)p2;
   return  x <= y ? ( x < y ? -1 : 0) : 1;
}
```

Memory Block Management

The following functions declared in *string.h* are used to compare, search, or initialize memory buffers:

void *memchr(const void *buf, int c, size_t n);
Searches the first *n* bytes of the buffer *buf* for the first occurrence of the character *c*.

void *memcmp(const void *s1, const void *s2, size_t n);
Compares the first *n* bytes in the buffer *s1* with the corresponding bytes in the buffer *s2*. The return value is less than, equal to, or greater than 0 to indicate whether *s1* is less than, equal to, or greater than *s2*.

void *memcpy(void *dest, const void *src, size_t n);
Copies *n* bytes from the buffer *src* to the buffer *dest*.

```
void *memmove( void *dest, const void *src, size_t n );
```
Copies *n* bytes from the buffer *src* to the buffer *dest*. In case the buffers overlap, every byte is read before another character is written to the same location.

```
void *memset( void *dest, int c, size_t n );
```
Fills the first *n* bytes of the buffer *dest* with the character *c*.

The corresponding wmem... functions, for handling buffers of wide characters with type wchar_t, are declared in the header file *wchar.h*[(*)].

Dynamic Memory Management

In order to make efficient use of memory, it is important for a program to be able to allocate and release blocks of memory dynamically during execution. The functions for dynamic memory management are declared in the header file *stdlib.h*.

A successful call to one of the memory allocation functions returns the beginning address of a memory block of the requested size. The return value has the type "pointer to void". The program can then use the allocated block in any way desired. When a block of memory is no longer needed, it should be released. All dynamically allocated memory blocks are automatically released when the program exits.

```
void *malloc( size_t size );
```
Allocates a memory block of *size* bytes.

```
void *calloc( size_t n, size_t size );
```
Allocates enough memory to hold an array of *n* elements, each of which has the size *size*, and initializes every byte with the value 0.

```
void *realloc( void *ptr, size_t n );
```
Changes the length of the memory block referenced by *ptr* to the new length *n*. If the memory block has to be moved in order to provide the new size, then its current contents are automatically copied to the new location.

```
void free( void *ptr );
```
    Releases the memory block referenced by *ptr*.

The following example uses `malloc` to allocate space for an array of 1000 integers:

```
// Get space for 1000 int values:
int *iArr = (int*)malloc( 1000 * sizeof( int ) );
```

These functions can be called as often as necessary, and in any order. The pointer argument passed to `realloc()` and `free()` must refer to a memory block that has been dynamically allocated, of course.

Time and Date

The ANSI C library includes a set of functions to determine the current time and date, to convert time and date information, and to generate formatted time and date strings for output. These functions are declared in the header file *time.h*.

The principal functions for determining the current time are:

```
clock_t clock( void );
```
    Returns the CPU time used by the program so far, with type `clock_t` (usually equivalent to `long`). The result can be converted to seconds by dividing it by the constant `CLOCKS_PER_SEC`.

```
time_t time( time_t *pSec );
```
    Returns the number of seconds that have elapsed since a certain time (usually January 1, 1970, 00:00:00 o'clock). If the pointer *pSec* is not NULL, the result is also copied to the location it addresses. The type `time_t` is generally defined as `long`.

The functions for converting and formatting date and time information are:

```
double difftime( time_t t1, time_t t0 );
```
    Returns the number of seconds between *t0* and *t1*.

```
struct tm *gmtime( const time_t *pSec );
```
Returns a pointer to the current Greenwich Mean Time as a structure of type struct tm, with members of type int for the second, minute, hour, day, etc.

```
struct tm *localtime( const time_t *pSec );
```
Like gmtime(), but returns the local time rather than Greenwich Mean Time.

```
char *ctime( const time_t *pSec );
char *asctime( const struct tm *ptm );
size_t strftime(char *dest, size_t maxsize,
                const char *format, const struct tm *ptm );
```
These functions generate a string representing the local date and time. strftime() accepts a format string to control the output format.

The function wcsftime() is a version of strftime() for wide-character strings, and is declared in the header file *wchar.h*(*).

Figure 6 illustrates the uses of the time and date functions.

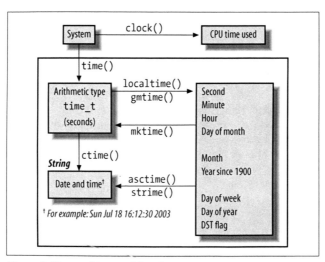

Figure 6. Usage of time and date functions

Process Control

A process is a program that is being executed. The attributes that a process can have vary from one operating system to another. For this reason, the process control functions work in ways that are specific to certain systems.

Communication with the Operating System

Environment
> In operating systems such as Unix and Windows, each process is started in an environment represented by a list of strings with the form *NAME=VALUE*. These "environment variables" can be read using the function getenv().

System calls
> The function system() invokes the system's command interpreter and gives it a command to execute.

Program termination
> A C program is *normally* terminated via a call to the function exit(), or by a return statement in the function main(). On normal termination, the following actions are performed:

> 1. Any functions that have been installed by atexit() are executed.
> 2. The I/O buffers are flushed and the files closed.
> 3. The files created by tmpfile() are deleted.

The function abort(), on the other hand, ends a C program without performing the actions just listed. This function does produce an error message announcing that the program was aborted, however.

The function exit() can be called with one of the constants EXIT_FAILURE and EXIT_SUCCESS, defined in *stdlib.h*, as an argument. In this way the program can inform its parent process whether it "failed" or "succeeded."

All of the functions described in this section are declared in the header file *stdlib.h*.

Signals

The operating system can send processes a signal when an exceptional situation occurs. This may happen in the event of a severe fault, such as a memory addressing error for example, or when a hardware interrupt occurs. Signals can also be triggered by the user at the console, however, or by the program itself, using the function `raise()`. Functions and macros for dealing with signals are declared in the header file *signal.h*.

Each type of signal is assigned a constant signal number and identified by a macro name. These include the signals listed in Table 41.

Table 41. Macros for signals in signal.h

Signal number	Meaning
SIGABRT	*Abort*: abnormal program termination, as caused by the `abort()` function
SIGFPE	*Floating point exception*: caused by an overflow, division by 0, or other FPU or emulation errors
SIGILL	*Illegal instruction*: an invalid instruction was encountered in the machine code
SIGINT	*Interrupt*: the break key (e. g., Ctrl-C) was pressed
SIGSEGV	*Segmentation violation*: illegal memory access
SIGTERM	*Terminate*: a request to terminate the program (in Unix, the standard signal sent by the `kill` command)

Other signals may be defined depending on the operating system.

```
int raise( int sig );
```
    Sends the signal *sig* to the program which called the function.

```
void ( *signal( int sig, void ( *func )( int )) )( int );
```
Specifies how the program responds to a signal with the number *sig*. The second argument, *func*, identifies the signal handler. This may be a pointer to a function, or one of the following constants:

- SIG_DFL   Execute the default signal handler.
- SIG_IGN   Ignore the signal.

The default signal handler terminates the program. If unsuccessful, signal() returns the value SIG_ERR.

The header file *signal.h* also defines the integer type sig_atomic_t. This type is used for static objects which can be accessed by a hardware interrupt signal handler.

Non-Local Jumps

Local jumps, or jumps within a function, are performed by the goto statement. The macro setjmp(), on the other hand, marks a location in the program (by storing the pertinent process information) so that execution can be resumed at that point at any time by a call to the function longjmp(). The longjmp() function and the setjmp() macro are declared in the header file setjmp.h.

```
int setjmp( jmp_buf env );
```
Saves the current calling environment (CPU registers and stack) in the buffer *env*, which has the type jmp_buf.

```
void longjmp( jmp_buf env, int retval );
```
Restores the saved environment, so that program execution continues at the point where setjmp() was called.

The program can use the return value of setjmp() to determine whether setjmp() itself was just called, or whether a jump to this point by means of longjmp() has just occurred. setjmp() itself returns the value 0, but after a call to longjmp() the apparent return value of setjmp() is the value of the argument *retval*. If *retval* is equal to 0, the apparent return value is 1.

Error Handling for System Functions

If an error occurs during a call to a system function, the global error variable errno is assigned an appropriate error code. The following three functions are used to provide the corresponding system error messages:

void **perror**(const char *string);   *Declared in stdio.h*
   Writes the text pointed to by *string*, followed by the system error message corresponding to the current value of errno, to the standard error stream.

char ***strerror**(int errnum);   *Declared in string.h*
   Returns a pointer to the system error message corresponding to *errnum*. The value of *errnum* is usually obtained from the error variable errno.

   The following two statements result in the same output:

```
perror( "OPEN" );
fprintf( stderr, "OPEN: %s\n", strerror( errno ) );
```

void **assert**(int expression);   *Declared in assert.h*
   This macro tests the scalar expression *expression*. If the result is 0, or "false", then assert() writes the expression, function name, filename, and line number to the standard error stream, and then aborts program. If the expression is "true" (i.e., not equal to 0), no action is taken and the program continues.

   If the macro NDEBUG is defined, calls to assert() have no effect.

Internationalization

The ANSI standard supports the development of C programs that are adaptable to language and country-specific customs, such as the formatting of currency strings. The ANSI library also provides two functions, the type lconv, and macros for dealing with locales. These are declared in the header file *locale.h*.

All programs start with the default locale "C", which contains no country or language-specific information. During execution, the program can change to another locale and retrieve locale-specific information. Since most applications do not require the full range of locale-specific information, this information is classified into categories, as shown in Table 42.

Table 42. Locale categories

Category	Portions of the locale affected
LC_ALL	The entire locale, including all of the categories below
LC_COLLATE	Only the functions strcoll() and strxfrm()
LC_CTYPE	Functions for character processing, such as isalpha() and the multibyte functions
LC_MONETARY	The currency formatting information returned by localeconv()
LC_NUMERIC	The decimal point character used by input/output and string conversion functions, and the formatting of non-currency numeric information, as returned by localeconv()
LC_TIME	Formatting of date and time information by strftime()

The following function is used to adapt a program to a specific locale:

```
char *setlocale( int category, const char *name );
```
The argument *category* is one of the symbolic constants described in Table 42, and *name* points to a string which identifies the desired locale for the specified category.

The name string may have at least the following values:

"C"
    The default locale, with no country-specific information.

""
    The compiler's native locale.

NULL

> setlocale() makes no changes, but returns the name of the current locale. This name can later be passed to setlocale() as an argument to restore the locale after it has been changed.

The following standard function groups use locale information: formatted input/output, character classification and case mapping, multibyte character handling, multibyte string handling, and conversion between strings and numeric values.

The following function can be used to obtain information for formatting numeric strings, such as the decimal point and currency symbol characters:

```
struct lconv* localeconv( void );
```

> Fills in a structure of type struct lconv with the values defined by the current locale. The members of this structure type must include at least those shown in the following example. The sample values in parentheses are those for Switzerland:

```
struct lconv {
//    Information for non-currency values:
   char *decimal_point;   // The decimal character
                          // (".")
   char *thousands_sep;   // The character used to group
                          // digits left of the decimal
                          // point (",")
   char *grouping;        // Number of digits in each group
                          // ("\3")
//    Information for currency values:
   char *int_curr_symbol; // The three-letter symbol for
                          // the local currency per ISO
                          // 4217, with a separator
                          // character ("CHF ")
   char *currency_symbol; // The local currency
                          // symbol ("SFrs.")
   char *mon_decimal_point; // The decimal point character
                          // for currency strings (".")
   char *mon_thousands_sep; // The character used to group
                          // digits left of the decimal
                          // point (".")
```

```c
char *mon_grouping;       // Number of digits in each group
                          // ("\3")
char *positive_sign;      // Sign for positive
                          // currency strings ("")
char *negative_sign;      // Sign for negative
                          // currency strings ("C")
char int_frac_digits;     // Number of digits after the
                          // decimal point in the
                          // international format (2)
char frac_digits;         // Number of digits after the
                          // decimal point in the local
                          // format (2)
char p_cs_precedes;       // For non-negative values:
                          // 1 = currency symbol is before,
                          // 0 = after the amount (1)
char p_sep_by_space;      // For non-negative values:
                          // 1 = space, 0 = no space
                          // between currency
                          // symbol and amount (0)
char n_cs_precedes;       // For negative values:
                          // 1 = currency symbol is before,
                          // 0 = after the amount (1)
char n_sep_by_space;      // For negative values:
                          // 1 = space, 0 = no space
                          // between currency
                          // symbol and amount (0)
char p_sign_posn;         // Position of positive_sign (1)
char n_sign_posn;         // Position of negative_sign (2)
char int_p_cs_precedes;   // For non-negative
                          // internationally formatted
                          // values:
                          // 1 = currency symbol precedes
                          // amount, 0 = currency symbol
                          // follows amount (1)
char int_p_sep_by_space;  // For non-negative
                          // internationally formatted
                          // values:
                          // 1 = space, 0 = no space
                          // between currency symbol
                          // and amount (0)
char int_n_cs_precedes;   // For negative internationally
                          // formatted values:
                          // 1= currency symbol precedes
                          // amount, 0 = currency symbol
                          // follows amount (1)
char int_n_sep_by_space;  // For negative internationally
                          // formatted values:
```

```
                                 // 1 = space, 0 = no space
                                 // between symbol and amount (0)
    char int_p_sign_posn;        // Position of positive sign for
                                 // internationally formatted
                                 // values (1)
    char int_n_sign_posn;        // Position of negative sign for
                                 // internationally formatted
                                 // values (2)
};
```

If the value of p_sign_posn, n_sign_posn, int_p_sign_posn, or int_n_sign_posn is 0, the amount and the currency symbol are set in parentheses. If 1, the sign string is placed before the amount and the currency symbol. If 2, the sign string is placed after the amount and the currency symbol. If 3, the sign string immediately precedes the currency symbol. If 4, the sign string is placed immediately after the currency symbol.

The value \3 in the strings grouping and mon_grouping means that each group consists of three digits, as in "1,234,567.89".

Index

We'd like to hear your suggestions for improving our indexes. Send email to
index@oreilly.com.
